# The Inward Path

# The Inward Path

*Contemplative Essays by*
**Nichiko Niwano**

*translated by*
Richard L. Gage

**Kosei Publishing Co.** • Tokyo

This book was originally published in Japanese under the title *Kokoro no naka no Sampomichi.*

Editing by EDS Inc., Editorial & Design Services. Book design, typography, and cover design by Becky M. Davis, EDS Inc. This book is set in a computer version of Palatino.

First English edition, 1989

Published by Kōsei Publishing Co., Kōsei Building, 2-7-1 Wada, Suginami-ku, Tokyo 166, Japan. Copyright © 1974, 1989 by Kōsei Publishing Co.; all rights reserved. Printed in Japan.

ISBN 4-333-01422-0
LCC Card No. applied for

*Contents*

*Outlooks and Attitudes* 11
Nichiren's Letter  13
Willful and Selfish  15
Forgotten Creativity  17
Learning to Live Better  18
The Importance of the Setting  20
Discontent and Dissatisfaction  23
Chance  26
Love for Children  29
The Importance of Persevering  33
Making Each Day Valuable  36
Angels of the Soul  39
My Inward Path  44

*Buddhism in Daily Life* 49
A Better World  51
Effort  54
The Pursuit of Learning  56
Good Health and Shakyamuni's
                Birth  58
Seeing Things Through  60
On Being Busy  62

Satisfied with Little 65
Setting and Achieving Goals 69

*The Meaning of Tradition* 73
Remember the Roots and Trunk 75
Respecting Our Heritage 77
Travel and Life 79
Punctuation Marks in Time's Flow 81
On Reading the Classics 82
Nichiren: Warmth and Determination 86
Emulating Dogen 90
Morning 95

*Seasonal Reflections* 99
The Bush Warbler 101
Crossing to the Opposite Shore 104
Cherry Blossoms 105
Flowers of Kyoto 107
The Northeast 109
Late-spring Verdure 111
Summer Thoughts 114
The Oze Highlands 117
Evening Showers 120
Winds 121
Flying to the Moon 123
The Night Sky 126
Life in the Snow Country 130
All Things New 134
In the Cold 137

*Thoughts on My Family* 139
My Father at Home 141
Mother, Our Sunlight 145

My Long-suffering Wife 148
Our Children 149

*Random Thoughts 153*
Experiencing Awe 155
Doing What I Dislike Doing 156
Calligraphy 158
A Matchmaker 159
Driving Safely 160
Becoming Like Children 161
Children's Songs 162
The Benefits of Fasting 164
Rubbing My Eyes in
                Wonderment 166

*Editorial Note*

In this book the names of all pre-modern Japanese are given in the Japanese style, with the surname first, and those of all modern (post-1868) Japanese are given in the Western style, with the surname last.

*Outlooks and Attitudes*

## Nichiren's Letter

The following passage occurs in a letter written by the great Japanese Buddhist priest Nichiren (1222–82) to a man named Nanjo Tokimitsu: "Have faith in the Lotus Sutra the way a hungry person longs for food, a thirsty person craves water, a lover desires to see the beloved, an illness demands medicine, and powder and rouge make women lovely. If you do not, you will regret it."

The purpose of the passage is to teach those desiring to follow the Buddhist way the attitude they must adopt toward religious faith. Nichiren is saying that faith must arise completely instinctively, the way a newborn infant seeks the mother's breast and the way lovers long to be with the people they love. But it is difficult for ordinary people to attain the state in which faith is as natural as this. If it were as instinctive to enter the way of faith as it is to want water when thirsty, there would be no need for religious leaders or houses of worship.

People turn to faith for a variety of reasons—

some because they are suffering and need help; others because, in looking back on the life they have led, they are overcome with awe and respect for the unknown they sense but cannot see. Most people, however, turn to religion for help in giving purpose to life. I believe the loss of meaning in living on which people frequently comment reveals how the spirit of religious faith has diminished in the minds of many people today.

The role of the religious leader is to waken the instinctive spirit of religious faith and to cause it to permeate all society in the most natural way possible. To carry out that duty, religious leaders must withstand many hardships. But it is a mistake to treat the instinctive faith Nichiren speaks of as an ideal difficult to realize.

Although it might seem that such faith is far removed from the realities of life, such a notion is contrary to the basic Buddhist teaching that the buddha-nature is inherent in every human being. This teaching means that hidden in the mind of each person is a need for religion as instinctive as the desire for water to quench thirst. The problem is finding a way to bring that desire into the open. In my opinion, the religious instinct is the loftiest of all human instincts: anyone who has awakened to the need for religious faith will have made a decision from which there can be no regression and will hold fast to it even in the face of universal cataclysm.

The infant's desire for the mother's breast and the patient's longing for the medicine that promises to cure are biological instincts. Religious faith, however, is an instinct of the mind, a spiritual instinct. Both instincts are essential to life. But biological instincts are periodic and subside when satisfied, as a person who has just drunk no longer craves water and one who has eaten to fullness has no further appetite for food. In contrast, once it has taken root in the mind, the religious instinct persists unaltered throughout life.

Ill people require medicine and thirsty people want water to satisfy their own needs alone. The religious instinct, however, inspires people with a desire to take their faith to as many people as possible and to save all society. Nichiren, other famous priests, and intellectuals have earnestly expanded religious faith into compassion oriented toward the salvation of all sentient beings. Observing their immovable faith makes it clear that professed religion that is self-serving and based only on response to the advice of an outsider or on the desire for some kind of gain is not the genuine thing. True religion is a faith instinctively desired from the depths of the soul.

Reading the teaching contained in this letter from Nichiren and slowly digesting its meaning showed me that the mission of the religious leader is to summon this desire in as many people as possible.

## *Willful and Selfish*

A little reflection will show that most of us are willful and selfish in many aspects of daily life. For instance, on days when I am going to do something I like doing, I wake early and leap from bed, bright and chipper no matter how cold it is. But when work that is progressing poorly awaits me, someone must wake me, and I am disgruntled that dawn has come so quickly. During the rush hour, when people must be at some distant place by a specified time, they are impatient each time they have to stop their automobiles at traffic signals. They forget where they are and shout out in anger if another driver, in an equally great hurry, tries to break into the line of traffic just ahead of them.

To one extent or another, practically everyone manifests such selfish attitudes, which even affect real estate prices. The people lucky enough to have bought land long ago, when prices were low, are now delighted at every upward leap in real estate values. The people who must buy land now, on the other hand, are outraged by spiraling prices, which they criticize as unfair. In short, human selfishness plays an important role in land prices.

If people humbly thought about it, the folly of willfulness and selfishness would become immediately apparent. But an objective view is very difficult to maintain when one is suffering or involved in some activity.

The historical Buddha, Shakyamuni, taught that delusion and enlightenment are one, meaning that selfishness and willfulness can lead to the search for enlightenment and wisdom. People who suffer because of their own delusions can discover things of value in their experiences. Indeed it is wonderful that people can learn flexibility and adaptability as a result of hardship. Since a life filled with delusions provides us many hints for the attainment of enlightenment and wisdom, we should be grateful. If selfishness and willfulness are interpreted in this way, they too can be of value to us.

## Forgotten Creativity

It is said that the number of people who can do nothing without relying on knowledge obtained vicariously from reading and listening is increasing. In other words, indirectly acquired knowledge is the authority, and people have forgotten how to make their own judgments and how to think independently. This may be another of the ills of our time.

I think the description "age of individualism" often applied to our time is merely wishful thinking. Each human being is unique and therefore ought to have his or her own distinct way of thinking, which in turn ought to generate creativity. But as I have suggested, this is not currently the case. One scholar has said: "The more culturally inclined people are, the less they use their heads." It is thought that we use only from 5 to 13 percent of the capability of our brains. The rising level of modern education should equip our brains to respond to any situation. In general, however, these well-educated brains are not used creatively.

Amazingly, people continue to rely almost entirely on what they have learned from books, not from experience and original thinking. I do not deny the importance of knowledge. But unless people see things with their own eyes, judge what they see and experience, and put their judgments—even if mistaken—into practice, they cannot be said to be living fully and creatively.

Each time I sense my own vicariously acquired learning flood my brain when I think of something, talk with someone, or sit down at my desk to write, it makes me shudder to realize that I too am one of the uncreative people. It seems to me that before we can make our own judgments and act on them, we must find a way to break away from excessive reliance on vicariously acquired knowledge. Of course, the problem would be solved if we so-called civilized people learned to use the 95 percent of our brains that is now idle.

## *Learning to Live Better*

People with no ideal in life experience a kind of lethargy. As more and more companies in Japan adopt the five-day work week and as the amount of leisure workers enjoy increases, we are being confronted with the problem of what to do with our free time. Many people fritter it away. Others do even worse and damage their bodies by spending their holidays eating and drinking. It would be much better if everyone devoted at least thirty minutes of a free day to thinking about and trying to understand the problems of human life and society.

In a book titled *Genshi Banroku* (A Late Record of Words and Intentions), the famous Confucian scholar Sato Issai (1772–1859) says:

Study in childhood is put to use in the prime of life. Study in the prime of life prevents senility in old age. Study in old age prevents decay, even in death.

Issai is telling us that there is no end to learning, that it must continue throughout life. Japan's Ministry of Education has been lauding the idea of lifetime education, but it seems strange to me that learning must be restricted to an institutional framework. In the past, when many people were illiterate, the situation was different. But now that practically everyone has a chance to acquire learning skills and the ability to absorb and understand, it seems better to abandon the position that education is something to be absorbed passively in a formal learning situation and to take the initiative and institute self-study programs to enrich our lives.

Never in history has the human environment been more conducive to such learning. If more people took advantage of their opportunities and gradually converted their idle time into fruitful time, there would be fewer old people condemned to senility, useless to themselves and burdens on others. Lives become useless not because of age but because people have ceased to progress through learning. This can happen to people of any age, and in the light of people's tendency to idle away time with no thought of improvement and development, I fear that the number of such fruitless lives will increase.

In late life, Shakyamuni Buddha said to Aniruddha, one of his closest disciples: "All the buddhas and world-honored ones are of the same kind. They are all alike in terms of precepts, liberation, and wisdom, but there is a difference in diligence. Of all the buddhas and world-honored ones of the past, I alone have attained the superior stage through diligence." In saying this, he was recalling that he was the only human being ever to attain buddhahood on his own, solely through diligence. The grandeur and importance of this idea is something we all ought to ponder.

If a universally revered man like Shakyamuni felt the need for constant effort in self-improvement, how much more is it incumbent on ordinary people like us to strive ceaselessly toward self-improvement. I often recite silently this line from an old poem: "He who makes no effort in youth and prime will spend old age in empty regret."

## The Importance of the Setting

Human beings are often strongly influenced by their environment. The mother of the great Chinese sage Mencius is said to have changed places of residence three times to give her son the proper environment for study. Certainly the setting plays a great part in the way children think and act. And adults too put their intentions into practice variously according to the nature of the environment they live in.

Sages of the past emphasized the influence of change of surroundings on the operations of the

## The Importance of the Setting

mind and acted on their concern, occasionally changing the sites where they trained in their search for enlightenment.

I was made vividly aware of the importance of environment on the two occasions when I took part in special training courses conducted for members of Rissho Kosei-kai at Ome, on the outskirts of Tokyo. The first time was in winter, when a heavy snowstorm had hit the city. The participants were all dressed in white robes, and the snow-clad world was all white. I felt completely changed as I and the others trudged toward the training center over an old, snow-covered country road.

The same training center made a vastly different impression on me when I took part in another session, this time during the summer. In contrast to the severity of winter, the summer there was gentle. The air was clean and refreshing, and the brilliance of the new foliage was dazzling. The early summer greeted us as a smiling mother greets her children.

Training itself was just as tough in summer as it had been in winter. The same kind of tension filled the air and engulfed us all in an atmosphere of fierce enthusiasm. Though there was never a moment's pause in demands for our full attention, to my own surprise I suffered no fatigue at all.

We were expected to be out of bed by five-thirty in the morning, but my eyes were open before then. I am noted for being a slow riser. There is usually a considerable interval between the time I wake and the time I actually rise from bed. Furthermore, even after I am on my feet, it takes me a long time to get ready for the day. This aspect of my behavior often irritates my family. But at the training center, I was up at dawn and dressed and washed in a twinkling. I was startled to see how a slight alteration in environment can work such a change in a person. Of course, the tension of the training program played a large part in my alteration, but the environment was important in maintaining that tension.

Just as I was affected by the training center atmosphere, a person walking through an entertainment district is likely soon to come to want to drink, sing, and have a good time. Or a person passing through the grounds of a Shinto shrine or Buddhist temple will be influenced to feel solemn and reverent.

In teaching that one is dependent on the setting instead of on the mind, Buddhism stresses the importance of the environment. Certainly, in modern times the influence of the environment can be cause for worry. It may be impossible to select one's environment as strictly and carefully as Mencius's mother, but we believers in the teachings of the Lotus Sutra feel we must alter our environment to the extent of making the home, the workplace, and the very street a setting for Buddhist discipline and training. This does not mean we can ignore actual conditions and devote ourselves entirely to training in these ordinary places. Just as Shakyamuni Buddha from time to time went apart to quiet groves to meditate, we should sometimes put ourselves in different surroundings and take a fresh, renewing look at ourselves.

From a slightly different viewpoint, today when the natural setting is being polluted and destroyed, the environment is of paramount concern to humankind. To save the natural environment from destruction, the emergence of more and more Buddhists is vital because Buddhism teaches that all things in the universe are part of an interrelated and interdependent whole and that the protection of some demands the protection of all.

## *Discontent and Dissatisfaction*

I once heard a story of a country district where the unpaved road became a quagmire whenever heavy rains fell, thus greatly incommoding the local residents, who repeatedly petitioned the municipal government until the road was finally covered with asphalt. But this led to greater traffic, with its accompanying noise, and to the fear of accidents. Moreover, the asphalt on the road affected the soil in the surrounding fields and harmed prized trees in nearby gardens. The upshot of this was that the residents who formerly had complained about the muddy unpaved road began accusing the authorities of creating a nuisance, when in fact nothing had been done but to comply with the residents' own repeated demands. Hearing this story reminded me of Aesop's Fables.

Similar stories abound. People have bitterly lamented the environmental pollution caused by a factory that they themselves requested be built for the sake of local economic growth. Other people who have opened their region to tourism have later come to grumble that tourists spoil the natural environment and mar what had been a pleasant place to live.

We are all selfish and willful in this way, and as soon as one vexatious grievance has been removed, another takes its place in an unending series. The human attitude toward freedom illustrates my point. As long as they are oppressed, human beings long for freedom. But as soon as they are free, they become frightened and begin looking about for a strong leader to guide and protect them.

The Weimar Constitution was considered a classic affirmation of liberty. But even as they were enjoying their liberty, the Germans became insecure and turned to the mad dictator Hitler for strong leadership. I have read the work of one historian who considers the Germans' insecurity about their liberty to be one of the major causes of World War II. When discontent and dissatisfaction grow to this extent, they are capable of leading to immense social destruction.

For some decades the Japanese have experienced extensive freedom and license. People who have the money to pay for it can get virtually anything they want. Any opinion, no matter how mistaken or one-sided, can be published. No one complains about what anyone else does as long as no law is infringed. Indeed, people are as ready to listen to the discontents and dissatisfactions of others as they are to scratch an itch. Never before in their history have the Japanese people experienced such almost unbridled freedom.

But at the same time the Japanese—especially the

## Discontent and Dissatisfaction

young Japanese—have felt pessimistic, bored, and unwilling to think seriously about things. Undeniably our time is beset with innumerable troubles. Most of the discontent and dissatisfaction voiced from day to day represents not awareness of these serious afflictions but only the sputtering complaints of people who feel constraint in the midst of freedom, think themselves discommoded in a world of conveniences, and have no understanding of sufficiency. These attitudes only intensify the frustrations from which people suffer.

Nonetheless, some people are aware of the need for informed severity on the part of leaders. Not so long ago, a pupil's article in a school paper caused a great stir in educational circles because it expressed the boy's wish that teachers would scold him so that he would feel he was being encouraged. I have heard that members of the Parent-Teacher Association—for a while after World War II vehement opponents of faculty members' interference in the affairs of children—did an about-face and shared this pupil's desire for discipline. These attitudes point to something that is, I believe, a key to an interpretation of the times in which we live.

Confronted with adverse conditions, any human being can face life and go ahead courageously and, with renewed courage and wisdom, overcome even the most hopeless, apparently irresolvable circumstances. That is the extent of the power inherent in the human psyche.

In favorable circumstances, however, we often lack the ambition to deal with even trivial, simple problems; progress ceases to seem meaningful, with the result that we wander aimlessly over the same ground looking idly at our surroundings, sighing, and voicing our discontent and dissatisfaction. That is precisely the state in which the Japanese, especially the young Japanese, find themselves today.

I believe that true freedom requires human beings to strip themselves of all delusion and deception, to face facts as they are, and to see things with the free and unclouded eyes of a child. People with such vision must then examine all the approaches to solving a given problem, abandon selfishness and grumbling, and pool efforts for the sake of progress. The new world we all seek can be created if we manifest this generous spirit of freedom and wisdom. To triumph over eternally budding and burgeoning frustrations, we must all try to define the way of life of truly free human beings no longer totally absorbed in the vacillating, shifting self.

## *Chance*

We use the word *chance* a great deal in everyday expressions, for example, when we say that something happened by chance, or comment: "As chance would have it . . ." The Japanese word *en*, which can be rendered into English as chance, is a Buddhist term meaning the kind of causal connection that results in a karmic effect. The way people interpret chance, in the Buddhist sense of a connection leading to a cause, often determines their whole way of thinking and even their fate.

## Chance

Even the most chance encounters can have serious outcomes, as the experience of Shakyamuni Buddha illustrates. After six years of ascetic practice in the mountains, Shakyamuni descended to bathe—for the first time in all those years—in the waters of the Nairanjana River, a tributary of the Ganges. Then Sujata, a maiden from the nearby village, offered him a bowl of milk gruel. When he had eaten this food, Shakyamuni felt that he understood the true meaning of human gladness. The joyful, carefree singing of a passing farmer gave Shakyamuni the feeling of having come into contact with simple, sincere human nature. This was the first time he had been enlightened to human life in some of its best aspects.

Having seen that the ascetic sufferings he had undergone in the mountains were useless in the search for enlightenment, Shakyamuni Buddha then came into chance contact with these people, and the encounters led to his meditation under a bo tree and finally to his supreme enlightenment. This illustration from the life of the Buddha shows the importance of chance in human life. If something had been vexing him at the time, the bowl of milk gruel might have done no more than assuage his hunger pangs, and the carefree song of the farmer might have been an irritation instead of a joy. But he was seeking enlightenment to the truth, and these simple chance events helped him follow the course that culminated in the attainment of supreme wisdom.

The point of this story is that the only way to attain enlightenment is to want to do so. Human beings can use whatever chances happen along to fulfill their missions in life, if they want to do so.

Tens of millions of people have seen apples fall to the ground from apple trees. Many of these people have been honored in their societies for wisdom and knowledge. But only Isaac Newton used this chance happening to formulate the law of gravity. We are all equally blessed with innumerable chances to seize the truth and make discoveries that could alter the future of humankind and the planet. Hints for such discoveries abound, but it seems to me that modern people lack the spirit of inquiry to make use of them. We have forgotten to be moved and excited by the things around us. We take things too much for granted.

In Japan it has been popular to talk of "defining things clearly." If this expression reflects a desire to fathom the unknown, I have no quarrel with it. But it seems to me that many people use the idea of defining things clearly as a compromise enabling them to settle for halfway measures. In other words, instead of recognizing the complexities of things and trying to examine them for deeper ideas and new truths, people are happy to make clear-cut distinctions that stop short of true profundity.

If everything in this world could easily be clearly defined, anguish would be at an end. But it is good that clear definitions are not always easy. It is precisely because things cannot be clearly defined that human beings have sought a better way, have repeatedly struggled for self-improvement, and have discovered clues to the solution of problems and relief of distress. By no means have all such clues been discovered. The world is eagerly in search of more of them than ever before in the long course of human history.

The desire to seek such clues is related to the will to develop one's own inner life. Perhaps the most important needs for humankind today are to pay close attention even to small matters—of future, present, and past—to make good use of all chance encounters, to be aware of the many things on which our lives depend, and to be constantly eager to make new discoveries.

Buddhism teaches that contact with the Buddha is essential to the enlightenment of individuals. But such contact can scarcely be made by people who fail to take notice of the things around them, dismissing them as unrelated to themselves and to their pursuit of self-development. As the illustration I introduced earlier shows, Shakyamuni Buddha was aware of everything around him and made use of all chance encounters in his pursuit of enlightenment. In this, as in many other things, I find in the Buddha's way of life a model for everyone's behavior.

## Love for Children

As a student I lacked the experience to understand the famous poem on parental love by Yamanoue no Okura (ca. 660–ca. 733), which appears in the eighth-century anthology *Man'yoshu:* "Why prize silver, gold, and jewels? Can they exceed the worth of children?" I thought it was extremely exaggerated and roundabout in expression. After having four children of my own, I came to understand precisely how the poet felt.

Each time I saw my children playing and romping, the light of their clear eyes shining bright, I thought how irreplaceable a jewel each one was. I am sure that most parents have that feeling. Nonetheless, nearly every day newspapers carry reports of the murder and abandonment of children. Even when abuse does not go that far, a growing number of parents neglect their children while satisfying their own material desires.

People who concentrate on acquiring material possessions and wealth may not value their children, and may think that since children are still unformed, they require little thought or attention. This attitude leads to neglect. Some young parents look on their children as playthings. In extreme cases, when the playthings become troublesome, such parents abandon or even destroy them.

Adults make an immense mistake if they consider children unformed and unobserving. The clear eyes of children see things that are invisible to us; they find surprise and delight in things adults have come to overlook. When I watch children going about their own activities, I realize that in saying no jewels can compare in worth with children, Yamanoue no Okura was speaking neither of the material value of precious stones nor of the love of a father for his children, but of the hopes older generations have for what their children will accomplish when they come of age and shoulder the burden of the future.

## Love for Children

I was recently impressed with the acute powers of observation revealed in something I read: "The wisdom to build the next age abides in children. It is mistaken to regard their lack of knowledge as lack of wisdom. . . . The modern age began with the surprise people experienced on seeing an apple fall or watching the lid on a kettle of boiling water rise. A new kind of surprise will open the coming age, which will be more than a continuation of the present."

Parents who regard children as possessions or playthings profane their innate possibilities. After birth, a child's first contacts are generally with its parents. From the mother's breast and the father's strong embrace, the infant becomes aware of being human. A child's character is not formed in school. The formation begins with the first physical encounters with parents, grandparents, brothers, sisters, and all the others present in the home. But parental contacts are certainly the most numerous —about 80 percent of all contacts in the case of nursing infants.

Many parents will hasten to say that a profound love, existing from the first, binds parents and children and that all children—except those born to people with no trace of parental feeling—grow and develop in the security of such love. In theory this makes good sense. But such a view leads to a mistaken interpretation of love and stimulates the tendency to treat children as toys. Parents often assume that their child returns their love from the moment of birth, but there is no evidence that this is so. Love between parent and child must grow and develop as the result of repeated contact. Only then does it become rooted.

Parents may love their children from the moment of birth or even from when the child is still in the womb. But such love is not strong; at least it was not in my case. When my eldest daughter was born, I experienced confusion, happiness, an awareness that the infant was charming, and complex emotions too subtle to describe with the single word *love*. I am sure that when asked I told people I loved my child; but my feeling was one-sided, vague, and not at all as profound as others seemed to expect it to be.

But over years of our getting to know each other, that vague feeling evolved into a firm, immovable love that became deeper and greater as the child grew. As this kind of love develops, the bond between parent and child comes not only to exist in the present but also to extend into the future. Further, parental love even expands to reach out to all children and the new world we hope they will build. As time passes, this greater love becomes the foundation on which a child's character develops.

As unexpected as the idea may seem, in terms of its breadth and depth, I think such love between parent and child is similar to the spirit of compassion taught by the Buddha. Love must be capable of the same boundless development as the Buddha's compassion, which extends to all living things.

The Japanese are generally eager to further their children's educations. But too often this desire compels the children to acquire masses of facts, while ignoring their education as human beings. Each time

I read newspaper stories of child abuse or abandonment or hear of parental love going astray to a child's detriment, I realize how great is the need for the Japanese to think about the social causes of these phenomena and about the greater kind of love that embraces not only children but also the future they face.

## The Importance of Persevering

When I was seventeen, I started training in kendo, the major goal of which is not to defeat an opponent but to cultivate self-control. Kendo is said to begin and end in courtesy, and its essence consists in developing the right attitudes for kendo training itself and cultivating other attitudes related to rules for daily life. It teaches modesty in all things and the importance of being able to persevere no matter what happens, not only in matters other people are aware of but also in things that are not immediately apparent.

Though I am embarrassed to admit it, my experience with kendo was marred by a failing on my own part. A student at the time, I decided I wanted to throw myself into kendo wholeheartedly and asked our teacher to permit me to live and work out at the training hall for the two months of summer vacation. He kindly agreed, and I did my very best for a while.

But after about a month had passed, I began to sense what I thought was a serious discrepancy between the ideal kendo I had envisioned for myself and the realities of training. I cannot deny that my attitude grew out of a mixture of conceit, immature thinking, and laziness. Nonetheless, though I had made a promise to train for two months, one day not long after I began entertaining these doubts, I left for home without saying anything to anyone.

On, I believe, the very next day, our teacher dashed to my house. Looking me straight in the eye, he said brusquely: "What do you mean by breaking your promise and going home before your time is up? You're the one who wanted to train for two months. Get back to the training hall at once. I gave my word to be responsible for you for two months. Till those two months are up, you're just like one of my own children. And you're coming with me this minute!"

Stinging from his words, I was immediately sent back to the training hall, where the course of hard training resumed.

One day not long after that, as if to drive his point home the more strongly, our teacher turned to me and said: "Remember, it's all over the minute you start breaking your word. Once people think you're not absolutely truthful, it'll take you ten years to regain their trust. Never forget that for a minute." And I never have.

His words are with me today. They and the hard training that followed my return to our teacher's house made me aware for the very first time that persevering means seeing things through to the end and that this is impossible as long as carelessness and dishonesty linger in the back of the mind. For

## The Importance of Persevering

the first time I came to understand the precious importance of seeing things through.

Though flawed by this mistake, my two months of training were soon completed, bringing me a sense of satisfaction and happiness that I have never forgotten. I would never have understood the joy that having persevered to the end brings, if I had been allowed to plead shallow understanding, to go on talking about the gap between ideal and reality, and to deceive my own conscience into letting me break off in the middle of the training course.

The lives of all the great sages of Buddhism are characterized by the ability to persevere through all things. Each of them contributed to the formation and development of the spirit of Buddhism while submitting himself to extreme hardship. I prize and respect the way they lived. Their experiences go far beyond my two months' perseverance in kendo training. But I believe that if each of us would cultivate an attitude of determined perseverance, even if it is only a small fraction of the persevering powers of the Buddhist sages of old, the world would be a very different place. Furthermore, the matrix of our lives should be the knowledge of how to become aware of the nature of society and human existence by persevering in the face of difficulties.

My kendo teacher told me that everything is over the minute a person starts lying and breaking his or her word. But today lying is all too often considered acceptable, perhaps because of the predominantly material orientation of society. It saddens me to see the extent to which untruthfulness and superficiality operate in human relations today. Widespread selfishness and self-interested calculation encourage reliance on deception and help create a society that permits it. In spite of the comfort and technical sophistication of contemporary society, the dignity of spiritual reason has been deformed and twisted practically out of existence.

In past ages, when human reason definitively characterized the lives of both individuals and societies, lying and deception were forbidden as equivalent to betrayal. Today, however, they are not only winked at but even recognized as essential expedients in daily living. I can only believe that this indicates the extent to which morality and religion have retrogressed in our materially centered society, which, having dulled human beings to the precious importance of the spirit, has caused flowers of evil to bloom under the name of abundance. Unless something is done to rectify this situation, humanity is headed for irrevocable destruction. We must rediscover as quickly as possible the forgotten importance of seeing things through and of staying spiritually free of lies and deceit.

## *Making Each Day Valuable*

Leonardo da Vinci said that a day well spent brings happy sleep and a life well lived brings happy death. And Nietzsche said that the sleep of a moral man is pleasant. The peaceful slumber following a day of all-out effort restores vitality and becomes a source of value for

## Making Each Day Valuable

the following day. Since a lifetime is only the sum of all the days lived, if all of us spent our days in valuable ways we could all achieve untold things.

Sadly, however, far from living in this way, too many people fritter away all their days. After a day filled with busyness and bustle, they are so disturbed by so many different things that peace of mind and sound sleep will not come. In our modern industrialized world, people tend to lose sight of meaningful living amid the complexities forced upon them by overweening materialism and by the flood of information that engulfs them, making them virtual slaves to their environment.

Some time ago, in the "Vox Populi, Vox Dei" column in the *Asahi Evening News*, I read something pertinent to this topic. The author said that for the people of Japan the first several years following World War II might be called the Age of the Stomach, since practically everyone thought only of finding something to eat to ease their chronic hunger. This was followed by the Age of Economic Growth, during which, intoxicated with rapid advances in many fields, people concentrated on the pursuit of material abundance. But, now, seeing that material well-being alone cannot bring happiness, the Japanese people are about to enter what can be described as the Age of Spiritual Values, which is certain to have a revolutionary effect.

I am in total agreement with this interpretation and with the remainder of the article, which said that the important thing in this new age is to determine the kind of nourishment needed to cultivate people capable of understanding spiritual values. In other words, how is spiritual hunger to be satisfied?

This is a question all of us must ask ourselves. For the sake of a new age, we must reflect on the profound significance of spiritual nourishment. This is especially true for the Japanese, who stand at the threshold of a new kind of society representing the culmination of everything they have experienced in the decades that have passed since the end of World War II.

But unlike the one we have known till now, the new world will not be a simple one in which financial security protects against hunger and work guarantees the gratification of material desires. To make the new world their own, all people will break their own ground and plant, cultivate, and harvest for themselves. It will be difficult to attain the best of the new age through no more than the frenzy and bustle of busy, fruitless days.

In a well-known passage in the *Analects*, Confucius says: "At fifteen, I determined to study. At thirty, I could stand alone. At forty, I was free of doubt about things. At fifty, I knew what Heaven meant for me to do. At sixty, I understood everything I heard." Even a person as great as Confucius needed sixty years to attain complete understanding. And those years were no doubt filled with steadily accumulating experience and with growing wisdom.

In comparison with Confucius's path, the one the Japanese have trod in perplexity and doubt since the end of World War II is still too short. I realize that many people will object that the pace of our age differs dramatically from that of the age of Confucius and that today no one can afford to spend fifty or sixty years attaining an ideal. It is true that the Japanese were able to get through the Age of the Stomach and the Age of Economic Growth at an accelerated tempo. But such speed will be impossible in the Age of Spiritual Values. This will not be a time for making short shrift of things because they are too much trouble or for always acting on the basis of established models.

The new age will not be one to pass through in the greatest possible hurry in the midst of maximum upheaval and change. Instead, in the new age we will have to examine all aspects of present-day life while trying to develop a way of living that can survive far into the future.

Fussing and fidgeting aimlessly through our days will no longer be tolerable. The time has come for us to begin dealing with the major issue of converting all our days—days equitably granted to everyone—into fruitful, valuable time. In my opinion, we can discover hints about how to do this and begin to make our own psychological preparations by reevaluating the fundamentals of Buddhism and the philosophies bequeathed to us by the sages of the past.

## Angels of the Soul

Since my student days I have been in the habit of underlining or copying out in notebooks especially striking passages in the books I read to impress them more vividly in my mind. Though it takes a little time and effort, copying a passage word for word gives one time to assimilate full meanings better than a single reading can and impresses deeply on the mind the profound reflection and diligence underlying even the shortest passages of truly significant writing.

I agree with the idea I read somewhere that we should read the books we like as ardently as we read love letters. Practically no one reads a letter from his or her beloved as if it were business correspondence to be glanced at and put aside. Instead it will be read again and again. The deeper the relation between writer and reader, the more attentive will the reading be. No word will be missed. Three or four interpretations will be made of the letter's meaning, and utmost attention will be paid to continuity, expressions, and nuances. The punctuation and the creases in the paper will be taken into account as if of great import. Even blank spaces will be thought to have meaning.

Of course reading an entire book in this ideal way is difficult, but I do think we should try to savor fully the meaning of those chapters or passages that make especially strong impressions on the mind.

Though I began copying out quintessential passages from great writings as an aid to self-examination when I reread them, on looking through my notebooks years later, I have found that great passages by people who understand the meaning of human life remain fresh and vital centuries and even millennia after they were written. I realize that these famous phrases and passages are not isolated luminous ideas or accidental remarks but represent the essence of the lives of the philosophers who wrote them. Here I should like to share just a few of the entries in my notebooks.

> The thorough clarification of the meaning of birth and death—this is the most important problem of all for Buddhists.*

This sentence from the *Shobo-genzo* (Eye Storehouse of the True Law) by Dogen (1200–1253), the founder of the Soto Zen sect, appears at the beginning of the *Shusho-gi* (The Meaning of Practice-Enlightenment), a book for lay believers compiled in 1890. In elegant Japanese, Dogen goes on to say:

> Since the Buddha [enlightenment] dwells within birth and death [delusion], the latter do not exist. Simply understand that birth and death are in themselves Nirvāṇa, there being no birth-death to be hated nor Nirvāṇa to be desired. Then, for the first time, you will be freed from birth and death. Realize that this problem is of supreme importance.†

In simpler terms, Dogen is saying that a person who has seen through the delusions of this world while still living in it realizes there is no such thing as life or death, since neither one nor the other is important. Such a person neither dislikes life and death as part of the world's delusions nor is attached to seeking the enlightenment of Nirvana. Such a per-

---

*Yuho Yokoi with Daizen Victoria, *Zen Master Dōgen: An Introduction with Selected Writings* (New York and Tokyo: John Weatherhill, Inc., 1976), p. 58.

†Ibid.

son has transcended both life and death and has therefore reached the supreme goal for human beings. We must diligently study the way of life that leads to the attainment of that goal. In this single concise passage, Dogen sent forth a call of utmost importance not to Buddhists alone but to people of all religious faiths.

Another of my favorite passages is this one from the Sutra of Forty-two Chapters: "On what shall I think? I shall think on the Way. What course of action shall I pursue? The course of the Way. What shall I speak of? The Way."

I need add no commentary to this passage, except to say that each time I murmur it to myself I am profoundly impressed with the precision with which it sets forth the ideal way to live.

> They . . . are as untainted with worldly things
> As the lotus flower in the water.

This passage from "Springing Up out of the Earth," chapter 15 of the Lotus Sutra, is noted in Japan for its connection with the religious name of the great priest Nichiren (1222–82): the *ren* of his name is written with the ideogram for lotus.

The lotus blossom rising above muddy pond waters is immaculate; it blooms unsullied by the mire in which it is rooted. Many people consider true nobility to lie in a solitary search for one's own realm, remote from the surroundings of one's time. But I disagree. I think true nobility means living in this world while consistently keeping oneself unstained by one's surroundings. It is easy to flee to a mountaintop or to a desert island to escape contamination with the filth of the world. It is much harder to stay among humankind, covered with the same dirt, and yet remain unsullied and preserve what one believes to be the correct way of life.

The *Dhammapada* (Verses on the Law) says that like the clear and calm water of a deep pool, the person who abides always in the Law is not attached to the transitory world and does not waver because of changing emotions but always has a tranquil mind. In these times, the tranquil mind is what we must all strive for; we must all strive to be like the lotus flower, pure in the muddy waters of a pond.

> Not forgetting danger in time of security, not forgetting decline in time of prosperity, not forgetting disorder in time of orderly government —by these are ensured the protection of the individual and the peace of the family and country.

This passage is from the famous Chinese classic the *I Ching* (The Book of Changes). Though the phrase "not forgetting disorder in time of orderly government" is often quoted as a warning against overoptimism, the passage in its entirety is more than a warning. It is a résumé of the way human beings and societies ought to live. The *I Ching* contains many noteworthy passages and, though written for the Chinese people of several millennia ago, holds a precious truth that comes across vast reaches of geography and time to make a fresh impression on the reader of today.

The essayist Genjiro Yoshida, who died some years ago, is one of my favorite authors. The following passage in his book *Waga Jinsei to Shu-*

*kyo* (My Life and Religion) made a deep impression on me.

> Words must be excellent interpreters of the soul. They must be a fragrance wafted from the soul. The soul resides in the innermost recesses of a forest of mystery. Its faint echoes travel through the grasses, caress the leaves of the trees, and like the humming of bees, quietly strike our ears. Words must be the symbols of the soul, the messengers of the soul, the angels of the soul. And we must be determined to cherish them.*

I never tire of this passage, no matter how often I read it. It seems to me that today our ears are dulled to the weight and reverberations of words. Today's ambiguous slang and coarse language are nothing more than conversational code.

People of the past, holding a different view of communication, spoke of the soul of words. Believing that each word was a reflection of the heart, they felt the need for care in their verbal utterances. I cannot help thinking that today we carelessly abuse these messengers of the soul called words.

## My Inward Path

I often long to stroll carefree along a path in the evening when the setting sun reddens the twigs of the trees. But for a city dweller like me, this is only a fancy. Thus I have imagined an inner path to satisfy my need.

---

*Genjiro Yoshida, *Waga Jinsei to Shukyo* (Tokyo: Daiichi Shobo, 1939), p. 372.

## My Inward Path

This path is utterly quiet· and very little frequented. Of course there are no irritating, noisome automobiles. Instead of echoing on pavement, my footsteps fall softly on leaves and earth. The scent of greenery is heavy from the tall grasses beside the pathway. Birds dart in and out among the branches overhead. Here and there the forest gives way, yielding to wider views, of a shrine in a grove, a thatched farmhouse, or paddy fields reflecting the setting sun, which reddens the sky as it slowly sinks behind a distant range of purple mountains.

Since none of these things can be enjoyed in the city—or anywhere else in Japan apart from fairly remote regions—my inner path must remain part of my imagination. But whenever I want to go for a walk I summon it up, and at once, not only scenes but also the feel of the clean air and the smell of the fields come to make my walk more pleasant. I see small white flowers floating up from the ground at the pathside and hear the rustling of fallen leaves as I pass over them. The sound of a distant threshing machine abruptly stops, and silence reigns except for the deep, remote notes of a temple bell tolling the arrival of evening. And still my inward path stretches on.

Though that path exists only in my mind, I feel more fortunate than people who have never lived in the country, since my experiences enable me to imagine such an inner path. Just after I entered primary school we went to live in my parents' home village in the mountains of Niigata Prefecture to escape the bombing in Tokyo. I am certain that my childish mind knew a great deal of sadness during the decade we lived in that village, but now only pleasant memories linger.

Ours was a simple childhood. With our playmates we roamed the hills and fields during the day, catching loaches in paddy fields or chasing locusts and forgetting that night would come. When we finally went home it was to sit around a fire crackling in the sunken hearth of the main room and eat our fill at the evening meal. We knew neither pride nor pretension.

I hear that many city dwellers today long for such a life, but I wonder if they could adjust to it even if given the chance. For example, could people who have always enjoyed the convenience of modern appliances be happy preparing every meal over an eye-smarting, smokey wood fire? Perhaps memories like those that help create my imaginary inner path are possible only if one has partaken of both the hardships and the happinesses of the past. Memory has a way of purging itself of unpleasantness as time passes, and fondness for the past grows deeper as it becomes increasingly certain that one can never return to bygone times and places.

The farther city dwellers are removed from nature, the more they long for it. And if that longing is hopeless, it is probably good to find consolation in the physical and mental repose to be had from an imagined inner path like mine.

The canyons of tall buildings, the vicious traffic, the noise, and the smog of Tokyo do not suit me at all. I often feel confused and completely out of place in the city I behold from my windows. Indeed most people must be uneasy in such an environment, which robs us of our humanity and reduces us to automatons. If I, having been born in Tokyo and having lived there far longer than I lived in the country, still consider a mountain village in Niigata my true home, how much more homesick must be the truly country-bred people who have moved to the city only recently.

The Chinese poet T'ao Ch'ien (365–427) has described the way of life that many city dwellers consider ideal:

> I live secluded in a place where few other
>     people live,
> Where there is no clamor of carts and horses.
> You ask me, "How do you stay calm here?"
> The farther one's mind is from worldly bustle,
>     the more it delights in a rural dwelling.
> I pick a chrysanthemum by the eastern hedge
> And gaze serenely at the southern mountains.
> The stillness of the mountains and the
>     setting sun are what I like best here.
> The birds are flying home together.
> I would tell you more of what I feel,
>     but I've forgotten the words.

The ideal is to recall the simplicity of country life while living in the noise and rush of the city and—no matter how busy the days—always to have a mental retreat where it is possible to think of nature and savor the truth far from the everyday world. If we could master the way of life set forth in the great Chinese poet's verse, there would be no need to escape to the country, because we would have a fresh world of nature always in our hearts.

My inward path is rich with the variety of seasonal change and is always near at hand. I enjoy walking along a raised path between paddies in the country where I used to live. The wind touches my cheek, and I inhale the sweet-sour fragrance of grass. As long as I live in the city, I intend to continue amplifying and improving my path of recollection and memories. Along the endless way of my fancy, flowers will bloom. Sometimes stars will flash in the limpid sky above; sometimes white clouds will sail by. Streams will murmur, insects will chirp in the thickets. . . .

*Buddhism in Daily Life*

## A Better World

In spite of material abundance, the world today is afflicted with many troubles, from deteriorating human relations and environmental desolation to the continuing inflationary spiral. In the face of these problems, it is time we devoted some thought to a reappraisal of the meaning of a world that is good to live in.

Whenever I attempt to determine the kind of action we must take to improve our world, I am always reminded of something one of my professors of Buddhist studies said: "The one way to create a world that is good to live in is to instill in all people an understanding of the principle that all things are causally interrelated and that all either stimulate or at least do not hinder the coming into being of all others. We are now studying together in this classroom because all things in the universe are ordered and preserve harmonious relations. Should that harmony be disrupted and should stars begin to collide in space, chaos would result—with obviously disrupting effects on our study. The Buddhist principle I have outlined is a formulation of the indirect causal links among all things, including human beings and their surroundings. If everyone in the world understood how deeply their own existence and happiness are connected to the existence and happiness of all other beings, our world would be a much better place to live."

But by their deliberate actions, human beings are constantly creating causes that *do* hinder the coming into being and happy existence of themselves, their fellows, and other creatures. For example, the National Railway Workers' Union in Japan conducts a yearly series of limited and general strikes that deprive tens of thousands, even millions, of people of essential transportation. Smoke, fumes, and polluted wastes from industrial plants threaten the health of everyone in their vicinity. Pollution has even contaminated Japan's seas to the extent that people all over the nation are afraid to eat fish and other marine products.

Strikes, traffic accidents, pollution, noise, price hikes, and so on all have deleterious effects on the lives of the majority of people and prevent the creation of a better world. Nor are such effects confined to the borders of a single nation. A war in one land strongly influences the fates of all other lands. A problem flaring up in one country sends sparks all over the world, disrupting the lives of people not at all directly connected with the cause of trouble.

In all these instances, whether the problem be strikes or pollution, the people causing harm are either unaware of or insufficiently concerned about the trouble their actions cause many other people.

It seems virtually impossible to live without even indirectly causing someone somewhere inconvenience or discomfort. Yet I am convinced that if we all fully comprehend the Buddhist teaching of universal causal interrelation and if we try to bear our interdependence with all other creatures in mind in everything we do, it will not be difficult to create a good world.

As my professor and mentor implied in expanding it to a cosmic philosophy, the Buddhist concept of interdependence encompasses everything from the individual human being to the vast expanses of the universe. To survive, we require light and heat from the sun, the air in the transparent envelope of atmosphere surrounding our planet, water, and our earth itself. In other words, we rely on the blessings of the world of nature. We are connected with infinities of both time and space.

While enjoying the blessings of nature with which we are endowed, we human beings live within a given social structure, produce and consume within a given economic system, and strive for order under a given political system. Such symbols of human society as culture, art, religion, and morality bud and flourish on the basis of social laws. The elements that hinder the creation of a better world are found not only in the often belabored political, economic, and social structure but also in the ways that individual human beings think and live. Clearly one of the fundamental causes of the trouble humankind faces at present is the loss of interest in thinking and living in ways that do not hinder others.

When asked why the world is not as good as it should be, most people point an accusing finger at politics, the economic system, or the social structure. Though prevalent, this attitude—which is based on a refusal to look to one's own faults and an attempt always to put the blame elsewhere—is not conducive to the creation of a better world. To bring realization of this ideal closer, all of us must understand the interdependence that binds us together and, shouldering our own responsibilities and duties, live in a way that hinders no one.

## *Effort*

For a Buddhist, the spirit of compassion is of utmost importance. The Sutra of Meditation on Amitabha Buddha says: "The mind of the Buddha is characterized by great compassion, an unconditioned compassion through which all sentient beings are gathered to it." Compassion entails pity and concern for all creatures, with no calculation of recompense. Buddhist compassion is permeated with the compulsion to help all beings and the inability to pass sufferers by without listening to their story and offering assistance. In contrast with Christianity, which is described as a religion of love, Buddhism is called a religion of wisdom and compassion. But wisdom, too, is a practical means of showing compassion, since it is a tool whereby people can be led out of delusion and into enlightenment.

Since compassion that transcends all other considerations has never been in greater demand than

## Effort

it is now, Buddhists have a mission to stimulate the growth and propagation of a spirit of pity and concern. I find a hint for a way of doing this in the final words Shakyamuni Buddha spoke before his death: "Monks, all things are impermanent. Diligently strive to find the Way for yourselves."

In other words, nothing in the world lasts, all things must pass. Therefore, we must remain firm in mind and, without self-indulgence, diligently continue our efforts to find enlightenment. In this exhortation to diligence, I see evidence of Shakyamuni's profound concern and compassion and his desire for everyone to accept that spirit of compassion and do all within their power to stimulate its further development. It is easy to speak of compassion, and few people will gainsay its worth. But human beings tend to consider themselves first and to think in terms of reward when it comes to putting compassion into practice in actual daily life.

The establishment of a welfare-oriented society is one of the major issues in advanced nations at the present time. Yet though much is said of methodologies and systems needed by such a society, for some reason little mention is made of the spirit of compassion on which it ought to rest. Outpourings of this spirit directed toward all things gradually change form to become acts of religious charity, which, without the consideration for recompense that characterizes some other forms of charity, originates in an unconditioned, compulsive desire to extend a helping hand even to total strangers. This feeling is suffused with the desire to live together with others in a society where happiness is shared by all and to expand the limits of such happiness to the fullest. A welfare society should rest on that spirit and on the efforts of people who wish to deepen and broaden its influence.

As the reign of the Indian emperor Ashoka in the third century B.C. illustrates, compassion is a key to peace. Having attained his throne through the horror of war, Ashoka repented and, after studying the compassionate teachings of Buddhism, resolved to use them in his governance. He renounced all belligerence and strove to build a realm filled with the joy of peace. When I think of how a monarch labored over two thousand years ago to solve problems very much like the ones we today find too difficult to solve, I am made aware of humanity's lack of effort in the centuries that separate us from Emperor Ashoka.

The chorus of angels in Goethe's *Faust* sing that they are able to save anyone who constantly strives. I believe that we must strive constantly to stimulate the growth of the spirit of compassion so that all humanity can live together in an atmosphere of mutual assistance.

## *The Pursuit of Learning*

In "Tactfulness," chapter 2 of the Lotus Sutra, we read: "Know, Śāriputra! / The Law of the buddhas is thus: / By myriads of koṭis of tactful ways / They proclaim the Law as opportunity serves. / [But] those who will not learn / Are not able to discern it."

In this passage, Shakyamuni Buddha tells us the

## The Pursuit of Learning

importance of studying his teachings over and over again. The two ideograms in the Chinese text translated here as "learn" simply mean "study," in the sense of studying a thing over and over until it becomes part of oneself and one's customary behavior. Out of curiosity, I looked up the Chinese word for *study* in a Japanese Buddhist dictionary, where I found three meanings: to master the Buddha's teachings correctly; to think of the Buddha's teachings by referring them to everyday life; and to repeat such study ceaselessly.

(I prefer to read Buddhist scriptures in the classical Chinese translations instead of in the annotated modern Japanese versions available, because careful reading of the old text enables me to savor the deep meanings that can be distilled into just one or two ideograms, as in the case of the two ideograms meaning study.)

After I discovered the profundity of the word *study* in the Lotus Sutra, I encountered a famous passage in the *Analects* of Confucius in which the same meaning is stressed: "Is it not a pleasure to learn and to repeat or practice from time to time what has been learned?" This statement means that the pupil must repeat the teachings of the master over and over till they become part of the pupil. As their deeper meaning is understood, the pupil will become more profoundly interested in them, and they will become a source of joy. Learning is genuine only when pursued to that extent.

As if to illustrate the importance of repeated effort in learning, the ancient Chinese devised the ideogram for *study* from two elements, one meaning wing and the other meaning white, and referred to the whole ideogram as "the continuous flapping of wings." For the sake of flight, the bird repeatedly flaps its white wings, just as we human beings must employ repetition in our study for the sake of attaining our goals.

My small experience with the word *study* in these two texts suggests that we should respect the venerable wisdom expressed in ideograms, which we tend to read mechanically and take for granted. Often they contain much that is pertinent to modern life.

## Good Health and Shakyamuni's Birth

In Japan the eighth of April is traditionally celebrated as the birthday of Shakyamuni Buddha. Of the various ceremonies performed to commemorate the occasion, the most familiar is the pouring of *amacha* tea (made from prepared hydrangea leaves) over small statues of the infant Shakyamuni, who stands pointing to heaven with his right hand and to earth with his left, symbolizing the remark he is said to have uttered at birth: "I alone am honored, in heaven and on earth."

A Japanese medical specialist who died not long ago had some ideas about the birth of the Buddha that arrested my attention. Another of the stories of the Buddha's birth tells of male and female *nagas* (dragon demigods who are protectors of Buddhism) who appeared from heaven when Shakyamuni was born; one of them poured warm water and the other cool water over the Buddha's body, which glowed golden. Endowed with the thirty-two physical marks of a buddha, his body illuminated the universe. That bath, in fact, is the origin of the custom of pouring *amacha* over small statues of the infant Shakyamuni on April 8.

Ordinarily a newborn baby is bathed in warm water only. But the specialist I mentioned pondered that double bath of warm and cool water and, investigating it scientifically, later used it as the basis of the health system he invented. Involving alternate warm and cold baths, his system has proved extremely effective.

In a book he wrote on his system, this doctor remarked that alternate warm and cold baths were probably customary at the time the Buddha was born and probably played a part in enabling Shakyamuni to live to the then very great age of eighty.

Though we tend to regard the Buddhist scriptures as remote from ordinary affairs, if we delve into their vastness we can discover many wise things that, apart from being great philosophical and psychological truths, are pertinent to what we think and do every day. We have much to learn from the doctor who found in the story of the Buddha's birth, usually regarded as mere legend, a truth that has proved useful to many people in a practical way. Moreover, his achievement not only indicates the need to examine Shakyamuni's profound teachings from many standpoints, including those of modern science and technology, but also shows how, as a consequence of such examinations, Buddhist teachings can find general applications in daily living.

## *Seeing Things Through*

The head temple of the Japanese Tendai sect is Enryaku-ji, on Mount Hiei, near Kyoto. For centuries, especially devout, determined priests of that sect have performed a rigorous form of ascetic training demanding that for one thousand days, over a period of seven years, they walk through valleys and across ridges to visit prescribed sites on Mount Hiei. A priest who actually completed that severe training wrote that he sometimes walked up to eighty-four kilometers a day and slept no more than two hours a night.

Hearing that these priests' legs grow stiff with exhaustion and that they frequently seem to tread the boundary between life and death for days on end, I realized that only a priest of the firmest, most unshakable faith could see such a pilgrimage through to the end. But those priests who have completed the training say that without undergoing something of that kind human beings cannot attain enlightenment to the truth that a vast force extending to the limits of the universe allows us to live.

Although I have never taken part in anything as severe as that thousand-day training, I am convinced of the importance of undertaking things and seeing them through to the end. In recent years, theory and idea take precedence over action in

## Seeing Things Through

many aspects of life, and their failure to produce anything concrete intensifies the sense of emptiness some people experience. It is important to attack a difficult issue directly and then to develop theories from that practical experience.

The *Dhammapada* (Verses on the Law) says: "If a man speaks many holy words but speaks and does not act, this thoughtless man cannot enjoy the life of holiness: he is like a cowherd who counts the cows of his master." This teaches the importance of practical action, which can be completed only with the determination to grit one's teeth if necessary and to see through to the end whatever one has started. Unfortunately, however, many people start things readily enough only to forget or abandon their resolve along the way.

It is not necessary to begin with very difficult, trying problems. Select something easy to address from among the many problems you experience. But then carry it out without deviating or regressing. For example, a short-tempered person might resolve to control his or her anger. Another person might resolve to read a passage from the scriptures daily. The important thing is to select a goal and then persist steadily until it is achieved.

Nothing can be mastered through theory alone. But adopting a course of action and sticking with it will inevitably bring results. Doing this is putting the Buddhist spirit to work in daily life. I am keenly aware of the importance of action seen through to completion in our modern world, in which theory alone often has the upper hand.

## On Being Busy

As our world becomes more sophisticated and more complex, most people find themselves constantly occupied and reflect their situation in such greetings as "Keeping yourself busy?" Though it could be described as the result of increasing affluence or of intensified interest in leisure activities, the demand for more free time—for instance, a five-day work week, which is slowly being adopted in Japan—can correctly be called the result of the need for a pause from all this busyness and a chance to regain a grip on one's humanity. Unlike other animals, human beings think and work not for themselves alone but also for family and society. Consequently, each of us requires free time to reflect on the important things we may be losing by allowing ourselves to be totally overwhelmed by the hectic activities of each day.

Interestingly, the ideogram with which the Japanese word for busy is written consists of two elements, one meaning "to lose" and the other meaning "the heart." Perhaps the people who devised this ideogram long ago were warning humankind of the danger of becoming too busy and heartless. Certainly, our excessively busy society today demonstrates heartlessness in such things as the frequent instances of young mothers abandoning their infant children.

Like Christianity, Buddhism is rich in parables, some of which relate to the question of labor and being busy. Shakyamuni Buddha often mentioned the smith as a symbol of the industrious worker. The smith sweats over flames, removing impurities from unrefined ores to extract pure silver. This indicates the way we should all strive constantly to remove from ourselves all contaminating elements so that we can become pure.

The *Dhammapada* (Verses on the Law) contains a pertinent passage to the effect that wise people live each instant to remove defilements from themselves. The way of life suggested by this passage recalls the farmer who must constantly weed fields to ensure a good harvest. And this in turn suggests the approach we ought to take toward being busy: everything we do should be done in the desire for self-improvement.

But even industrious smiths pause in their work to appreciate the gleaming pure silver they have extracted. And farmers stop weeding, sit, drink a cup of tea, and enjoy the clouds sailing by overhead. There are other ways to introduce a moment of rest into the busiest schedule. The worker in the cold, impersonal atmosphere of a modern office can stop for a while to watch the throngs passing by on the street below or to read a few pages from a favorite book. Such activities are not escapist; in the forbidding desert that constitutes reality in much of contemporary life, they are oases where we may wipe the sweat from our brows, rest, and reflect.

How we use our leisure time is crucial. It cannot be fruitful or have a restorative effect if we waste it in such tiring, even physically harmful, pursuits as gambling or drinking from morning till night.

We should remember always to maintain a balance between work and rest. We should also remember to use at least part of our leisure time for reflecting on the significance of our actions. The Swiss author Carl Hilty (1833–1909) says in one of his works that the correctness of human truth depends on the way a person carries out minor acts. He adds that the way we perform these acts depends on a certain moral background, whereas, on the whole, justice may be no more than habit or pure craftiness and so never fully elucidates the human personality.

When involved with the peace movement or social action, we often use such high-sounding terms as "world peace" and "the ideal society," but we ought to stop and ask ourselves seriously whether we have trained ourselves sufficiently in all minor matters to be able to speak loosely about such major goals. Peace itself depends on the small acts of each individual human being. We must not let ourselves be so dazzled by the ideal that we lose sight of the groundwork without which the goal cannot be reached.

I have already pointed out the importance of reflection on our actions. I believe that sincere reflection reveals the extent to which we are carried away with all kinds of trivial thoughts and ideas. Sound reflection helps us put all those thoughts in order, systematize them, discard what is useless, adopt what is good, and in this way draw up a plan for living.

In the scurry of busy days, we lose sight of ourselves. We fill even our leisure hours with busyness and activity. Distracted by superficialities and blinded by the glory of the ideals themselves, we allow our work for such causes as peace and a better society to become empty and mechanical.

We are all busy. But in the midst of our activity, we must minimize trivialities, keep a firm grip on what is pure in our natures, and above all guard against losing our hearts. To cultivate in each person both truth and the desire to live in the way I have outlined is conducive to peace and the ideal society.

## Satisfied with Little

I stopped eating breakfast about twenty-five years ago. People sometimes asked me whether at that age I did not need three meals a day instead of two or if eating fewer meals affected my health. I do not advocate just two meals a day for everyone. I do not force my practice on others or try to disregard custom. It has simply been my experience that eating only twice a day is the best way for me to stay fit.

Once when I was receiving advice on maintaining my health, I was told that eating breakfast can actually be harmful. Though I doubted my ability to tolerate hunger, I decided to give the two-meal system a try. After all, if I saw that I could not survive on two meals a day, I could always go back to eating three. After the first few days, however, I felt wonderful. Gradually extending the regimen a day at a time, I have done without breakfast now for over two decades, and it has become a habit.

The advice I received was based on a theory that in the morning the body's excretory organs are active and that eating at that time would dull them and is unnecessary, since sufficient energy has accumulated from the previous evening's meal and a night's sleep.

I do not know whether medical science supports this view. Judging from vociferous assertions that going without breakfast is harmful to school children, many people consider the theory I embrace mistaken. Nonetheless, it works well for me. In the first place, since I stopped eating breakfast, I have suffered no ill health. In the second place, the time and mental latitude I gain from not eating breakfast have proved highly advantageous in daily life.

I tend to sleep late. Not bustling about to be on time for the morning meal gives me a few extra moments to think, read, and make notes on passages that strike me as interesting or valuable. And this in turn has an amazingly good effect on the rest of my day. When I get hungry, between ten and eleven in the morning, I find my mind is clear and alert enough for me to work more efficiently and be at my best for writing or conversation. The greatest advantage of omitting breakfast comes at this time of the day, when I am at my best mentally and physically. Not surprisingly, I have a tremendous appetite for lunch, which tastes delicious and is all, I am sure, converted into blood and muscle to help me remain in good condition.

Customs of long standing may be well founded, but sometimes they are the result of mere force of habit. When that is the case, they should be reevaluated. Human beings eat to satisfy hunger and to obtain energy. From these physical needs have

## Satisfied with Little

arisen both a large variety of cuisines and the custom of eating three meals a day. Eating can be a source of great pleasure as well as a way to end hunger. Cooks take great pains to enhance that pleasure by making foods as delicious, nutritious, and satisfying as possible.

Mere habit nonetheless has led human beings to believe that they must eat at established mealtimes whether they are hungry or not. And when we eat without appetite we merely shovel food into our mouths, savoring nothing at all. Not really wanting what is put before us, we waste food. The bigger the meal, the greater the waste.

Buddhism teaches that we should desire little and be satisfied with what we have. The poet Kenji Miyazawa (1896–1933) has given this philosophy beautiful poetic form:

> Strong enough in body
> To bow to neither rain nor wind, nor snow
>     nor summer heat;
> Desireless and wrathless, smiling always softly;
> Living on four measures of rough rice, bean
>     paste, and a few vegetables each day;
> In all things restraining emotion,
> Observing and listening well, and
>     understanding.
>
> . . . . . . . . . . . .
> That is how I want to be.

But today the idea of wanting little and knowing satisfaction with what one has is largely forgotten. In the Sermon on the Mount Jesus says: "Look at the birds of the air: they neither sow nor reap nor gather into barns, and yet your heavenly Father feeds them. Are you not of more value than they?" (Matthew 6:26). People capable of understanding the wisdom of this passage must put into practice at work and at home the philosophy of wanting little and being satisfied with what one has.

In India and Africa millions suffer poverty and starvation. Photographs of Indian and African children with blank looks in their eyes as they beg for food are heart-rending. The Japanese knew hunger and deprivation during and after World War II, and many of them died of starvation in Siberia and the South Pacific. The Japanese must do what they can to help peoples now facing similar tragic plights in other parts of the world. For example, it would pose no crushing burden on anyone to give up one meal a day and donate the money saved that way to the starving. The food crisis must be dealt with globally and with serious measures.

As life improves, people tend to forget past sufferings. Most Japanese who experienced them are willing to talk of the horrors and hardships of war, but often the talk goes no further than complaints and regrets. Yet those memories should inspire us to sympathize with and help others suffering now.

The people of Japan are in a position to help today. And if they would, the world would be warmer and truly united in the richest sense of the word. If all peoples everywhere put their minds to it seriously, we could overcome the food and energy shortages that threaten us. With everyone's cooperation, this can be done in modest ways that tend to be forgotten or overlooked.

As the great Japanese Buddhist priest Kukai (773–835) said: "Buddhism is not far off but close, in the heart."

## Setting and Achieving Goals

In the various situations in which they find themselves in life, human beings often allow their egos to show too much, or assert themselves more than is proper. As a result, personal relations suffer; activities that would entail no difficulty at all if approached coolly fail to succeed because the people involved become emotionally upset. The ego of a person who repeatedly devises ways to keep his or her mind empty of self is not ruffled when something untoward happens. Worries and difficult problems do not get the best of a person whose mind is always calm. Constant mental vexation, on the other hand, can spoil a person's appearance and sometimes even lead to physical illness.

Maintaining a flexible, open mind is important in all things. Even a tiny drop of water sours if allowed to stagnate. But the human mind cannot be allowed to stagnate: it must accommodate itself to changing circumstances. A passage in chapter 16 of the Lotus Sutra teaches the value of a straightforward and pliant attitude, and the same teaching is found in the New Testament in the Gospel of Matthew: "Blessed are the meek, for they shall inherit the earth."

But modern society is so full of things that cause confusion and trouble that maintaining a meek and flexible attitude toward life is far from easy. This is why I constantly caution myself against trying to do too much at one time. In any case, I am not adept at managing a number of things at the same time. To guide me in handling well the things I do undertake, I have set myself a motto: Keep Your Mind Flowing.

Starting many different projects usually means that none of them will be successfully completed and that a vexing sense of having accomplished nothing will persist. To avoid that, I prefer to undertake only those projects that I know are within my limits and then devote myself wholeheartedly to their completion. I have no regrets if I take a long time doing what I set out to do. It seems perfectly acceptable to me to deal calmly with matters, facing them as they are, without reading into them more than is there and without hurrying.

My recent contacts and conversations with young people have impressed on me the difficulty of living in the modern world. No matter how long we talk, they never seem to run out of troubles. Though these discussions make the distresses inherent in modern society painfully apparent, I cannot help feeling sorry that vigorous young people fail to do no more than stand wearily, arms folded, in front of their wall of sorrows. I do not think they are cowards or escapists. As is, in my view, characteristic of young people today, they simply do not know how to begin addressing the multitude of topics and tasks of modern society.

Throughout history, young people have been characterized by the desire to do perfectly whatever

*Setting and Achieving Goals*

they undertake. But it must be remembered that human civilization has usually developed less by sudden brilliant achievements than by steady, step-by-step climbing of the rough and hilly way. Our forebears steadily conquered one problem after another to create human civilization, moving much in the fashion of the ox in this poem by Kotaro Takamura (1883–1956):

> The ox goes slow
> But straight, wherever it wants—
> Meadow or mountain,
> Road or river.

How much more valuable in our time of apparently insurmountable difficulties is the cautious, steady method of the ox! Instead of letting the mind run loose in a search for perfection from the outset, it is better to set a goal and then move toward it step by step. As one effort crowns another, before the person is aware of it, the goal will be reached.

Even if the task must be left incomplete, the person whose efforts have been focused and who has done his or her best to finish it need have no regrets. Others will come along to take up where that person left off and see the work to conclusion. For some people it is good to hold the torch of ideals aloft. For some it is good to look thoroughly into a great many problems. But no progress can be made by simply standing still. Steady forward movement is the important thing.

My motto Keep Your Mind Flowing means setting goals, selecting the most practical methods to achieve them, and then working till the goals are reached. Without undertaking too much and without straining, even if I am slow, I prefer to walk along at my own pace, steadily, like the ox. Of course, I insist that maximum effort be made; I do not advocate careless indifference. But instead of trying to reach too far and then worrying afterward why things did not turn out as I wanted, I think it is better to set goals and reach them one by one in a life that is free of regrets. Keeping the mind flowing in this way leaves no room for emotional turmoil and inspires the attitude Jesus commended in those he described as the meek.

In the Majjhima-nikaya (Medium-length Discourses), it is said: "Neither pursue the past nor wait for the future." This is excellent advice for living today. What is in the past is over; what is in the future is a phantom that has not arrived. Without spending too much time reminiscing about the past and dreaming of the future, we should go about our lives with a steady, unperturbed eye for the present. Of course, paradoxically, living in the present is the same thing as pioneering the future.

The people of the past dreamed of a future filled with brightness and hope. The dire threats that loom over the world have filled our future with despair. Bringing light and hope back into the future is the task of those of us living now. It is one of the hardest tasks people have ever been called on to perform. Some will falter under the load. Some will abandon hope. But we can help dispel gloom and contribute to the improvement of our world if all of us set our own goals and earnestly—even if slowly—move steadily toward their attainment.

*The Meaning of Tradition*

## Remember the Roots and Trunk

In ancient India, Buddhist monks made their robes of discarded rags, washed and then sewn together in a patchwork pattern. Of course, a lack of looms to weave large pieces of cloth may have contributed to the custom of piecing rags together, but the primary motivating force was the desire to make use of available materials, no matter how small. Following this tradition, the *kesa*, the outer robe worn by Japanese Buddhist priests, is made of small bits of cloth pieced together in a patchwork pattern.

In a similar way, tradition can be kept alive in many areas of life; lifestyles should be evolved by applying new ideas and techniques to a framework of the old. In other words, tradition is our civilization's roots and trunk. A look at the way many people in Japan live today suggests that roots and trunk are being forgotten while people concentrate on branches and flowers. But no real branches and flowers can grow without roots and trunk.

Young people today dismiss things inherited from the past as useless and unnecessary and welcome nothing but the new. Eager to learn from other countries, they tend to slight the traditions evolved over the centuries at home. Of course, it is good to learn from other countries, but before doing so we ought to reexamine and make use of the heritage of our own tradition.

Today's throwaway culture is indicative of the way the Japanese people have adopted an American fashion with less than satisfactory results. It is now considered sensible to buy new things, use them till they are out of date or damaged, throw them away, and buy something new again. People no longer fold up and save wrapping paper or dismantle and keep cardboard boxes for later use. There is no room in the modern home to store such things. Instead of being repaired, slightly damaged articles are tossed out and replaced. One result of the throwaway culture is such a tremendous increase in the volume of rubbish that cities are sometimes nearly paralyzed when disposal facilities prove inadequate. Furthermore, unbridled consumption results in shortages of raw materials and rises in prices of consumer goods.

But the gravest harm done by indifference to the things we use is the desolating effect on the human mind and heart. People tend to look lightly on everything, including life. And this helps account for the cases of child abandonment and child murder, which occur with distressing regularity. Despising tradition, young people equally despise the wisdom of the old, who might be able to do something to stem this dreadful tide of callousness.

Our duty in life is not to discard all the things our forebears labored to produce and refine as part of our common cultural heritage but to use the many old things that can and ought to be used, to add what we can to them, further refine the results, and pass the modified tradition on to posterity.

Tradition—the roots and trunk of our way of life—did not come into being fortuitously. It grew from the wisdom and efforts of our ancestors. It is our cultural inheritance and must be the basis on which the culture of future generations can evolve. The good things in tradition have been handed down over many centuries, and we must spare no effort to leave those good things to posterity.

The contemporary Japanese practice of living for the flowers alone without considering the rest of the plant is, in the truest sense of the word, rootless. It is futile, since it starts at zero and can do nothing but end in zero. Most of the fads that swept through Japan in the years following World War II enjoyed a moment in the limelight but vanished without a trace. It makes me sorrowful to think how much precious time we have frittered away in pursuing such phantoms and how much damage we have done by forgetting our traditional heritage.

## *Respecting Our Heritage*

On a trip to Japan's northernmost island, Hokkaido, a few years ago, I stopped to admire a memorial tower erected by local citizens to celebrate the centennial of pioneering there. As I looked at the tower, I could not help thinking the forebears of today's Hokkaido residents would be amazed to see the shining high-rise buildings of the capital city of Sapporo, on a plain that not so long ago was an uninhabited wilderness. The tower, on which are engraved words expressing gratitude for the toil and sweat of the people who laid the foundation of modern Hokkaido, is significant in that it reveals the respect the people there have for the work and achievements of their predecessors. But it seems to me that despite symbolic gestures like erecting that memorial tower, we tend to forget much of the heritage our ancestors have left us.

I am speaking specifically of the splendid traits the Japanese have inherited from the past and of which they can be justly proud. Some of those traits are kindness, eagerness to avoid causing other people trouble, a capacity for hard work, and concern for the well-being of parents. The Japanese always take the opinions of others into consideration in their actions. It is a mistake to interpret this as a negative trait, since that consideration rises from an unwillingness to cause trouble. The Japanese readiness to exert effort in their work derives from their ancestors' dislike of falling behind and the culturally creative urge that stimulated constant self-improvement.

Not all of the things inherited from our forebears can be used without alteration in modern life. It is important to prize not the actual practice of the past but the spirit behind it. As an old saying has it:

"Follow not the footsteps but the goals of the people of the past."

Today Japan's young people tend to scoff at ideals of filial piety as hopelessly outdated. It is not my intention to suggest that we turn back the clock and reinstate the morality that was current decades ago. But in this age of mechanization, with its emotional sterility, I consider it dangerous to be too hasty in discarding the spirit and characteristics the Japanese enjoy as a part of their ancient tradition.

As the mechanization of society advances, the spirit and courage that support humankind deserve increasing respect. If these things are abandoned, human beings may become the servants of the machines they have created. Remembering and prizing the good traits passed down to us by our ancestors can prevent that. Looking up at the Hokkaido memorial tower and recalling the spirit of the pioneers it celebrates, I was deeply impressed with the need all of us have to reevaluate the fine things we have inherited from the past.

## Travel and Life

Whenever I think about traveling, these words come immediately to mind: "For hundreds of ages, the sun and moon continue their journeys; the coming year too is a voyager." These lines, from the opening of the famous poetic diary *Oku no Hosomichi* (The Narrow Road to the Deep North) by Matsuo Basho (1644–94), seem to express tersely the nature of life.

Though traveling to see the sights or enjoy a restful holiday is easy now, for the people of the past it was a kind of discipline involving great hardship. Walking day and night over twisting roads and steep mountain paths, people of those times may have thought, like Basho: "Travel involves hardship and my route is through remote country. I am resigned to the impermanence of all things, and if I die along the way, it is only the will of heaven."

No one tells so well or in so moving a fashion as Basho the way the Japanese people of long ago regarded travels that were more trying than anything we can imagine. Basho himself lived under trees and slept on stones, as did religious ascetics, and to one degree or another all travelers of his time shared the same experiences.

Amid the conveniences of life today, we have no conception of what those experiences were. Nonetheless, in the spirit of the proverb "Follow not the footsteps but the goals of the people of the past," we ought to attempt to understand the attitude of travelers in the past so that we can revise our own appreciation of travel.

When travelers think of themselves, their families, or human life in general during a trip, fresh ideas fill their minds. A sadness may well up in their hearts. Travel should do more than relax and offer a change of scenery. By acquainting us with unfamiliar places and sights, it should enable us to take a fresh view of familiar things. It should enable us to take a new look at life itself.

## Punctuation Marks in Time's Flow

New Year's Day, the vernal equinox, and other annual observances punctuate the flow of time in a year. The shift from one year to another that separates December from January makes an especially strong impression, refreshes the mind naturally, and invigorates in a wonderful way. All the other punctuation days in the course of a year have a vitalizing and restorative effect.

On a larger scale, a lifetime too is punctuated—by such things as coming of age, marriage, anniversaries, and so on. And the twenty-four hours of a day are divided into periods by mealtimes and breaks, when people relax and take refreshment that enables them to continue their work renewed and revived. In Buddhist terminology, these breaks can be called *hoben*, or expedients, bringing about a change of mood and a change of attitude.

Though it would be excellent if we could, not all of us are able to go through life, a year, or even a day completely fresh and at our best. We all occasionally become lazy and use time prodigally. And the well-placed time punctuators our forebears arranged for us in the temporal flow are the reminders we need if we are to get a fresh grip on life.

The people of the past used astrology, meteorology, wisdom, and experience of the shifting seasons to establish these markers in time. But in the modern urban way of life, things have changed so much that people gradually lose track of the meanings of the old time demarcators and, sadly, pay little attention to them. This is another instance of how tradition is being forgotten.

If traffic lights were eliminated from the highway system, chaos would result. Similarly, if these time delineators are forgotten, riot is likely to ensue. These punctuations in our years and days resulted from the wisdom of people of the past and are intended to serve as brakes on our impulses and to enable us to walk safely and with fulfillment down the path of life. We ought to prize these aspects of our traditional heritage more highly.

## On Reading the Classics

I enjoy nothing so much as reading, whether it be indoors with the sun streaming in during the spring, outdoors under a green tree in summer, someplace where I can hear the insects chirp in the fall, or wrapped in the congenial warmth of a *kotatsu*—a low quilt-covered table with a heater under it—in winter. Before I discuss the kinds of things I like to read, I should like to say a word about the best places for reading.

The ancient Chinese held that the ideal places to read books or polish one's prose are on horseback, in bed, and in the toilet.

I can readily imagine the joys of getting lost in a good book while riding through a country field on the back of a gentle horse. But in the modern world of highways, vans, and trucks, imitating the ancients in this habit could be fatal. This way of read-

## On Reading the Classics

ing must be eliminated for almost all of us today.

Any devotee of reading knows the relaxation of lying in bed, with a bedside lamp glowing, and forgetting the troubles of the day by delving into a book before falling asleep. But for me this too is no longer possible. When my wife and I had our first child, I had to give up reading in bed because the baby slept in the same room with us and the bedside light might have kept her awake.

The toilet is the ideal place to read and reflect in silence, free of the need to worry about disturbing anyone else. For a long time I savored the joys of being a bed and toilet reader. But since reading in bed has been denied me, of the three places recommended by the ancients, the toilet alone remains to me. And even today, no matter how short my stay there, I am intolerably bored unless I have something to read.

I heard that the late novelist Shugoro Yamamoto, who was a toilet reader too, was once reduced to perusing with great care the two sides of a bank note because he had forgotten to take a book to the toilet with him and could not tolerate being there with nothing to read. I find the image of him digging through his pockets in the hope of finding reading matter very amusing. Nonetheless, I am as addicted to the habit as he and am now planning the perfect toilet for reading in the house I may someday build.

My reading matter is almost invariably the classics, especially works on history. Some people argue that my material is too difficult and ask me if I dislike contemporary writing. Not at all. I realize that the writings of our own time are filled with the insecurities and worries we all share and that such writings ought to be explored for hints on how we should travel the path of life. I certainly do not despise or underrate contemporary literature.

Nonetheless, I limit myself largely to the classics because they are part of our human heritage, have withstood time's winnowing, and deal with elements that are most fundamental to humanity. We delude ourselves in thinking that humanity has progressed tremendously over the ages. Civilization itself has of course made advances at a rapid rate, but our spiritual growth is open to question.

When I read books written centuries or even millennia ago by great people of religion, philosophy, and poetry, I sense echoes of their lofty spirits. The immutable truths I discover in their opinions and words strike my heart.

Historical periods can be characterized by incredible error, as one can quickly discover by glancing at books by militarist thinkers printed in Japan during World War II. When such works were first published, I was too young to read them. Now, reading through some of them in secondhand bookshops, I am amazed that the Japanese of the time failed to notice anything unnatural in the biased ideas of those writers. But as I think this, I ask myself whether people in the future will not say something very similar about currently popular writers and their bestsellers, many of which are fated to be forgotten as time goes on.

In the past too, though perhaps not to the same extent as today, many books were written, read,

## On Reading the Classics

and forgotten. The useless ones were culled out over the ages, and only those of true value have survived. These are the classics. Though the opinion of a particular age may have been mistaken in many ways, human history, measuring with a larger scale, has been wise enough to select unerringly those things that contribute to the creation of an outstanding heritage. That is why I love the classics. All of them have something which we should heed, something from which we can learn.

Reading is, as I have indicated, a source of supreme joy. But a great gulf separates reading the classics from whiling away an hour with a work of popular fiction. For one thing, the obscure and archaic words and expressions in classical works can be irritating obstacles to rapid reading. Often, when forced to plod through one of these works word by word, impatient people want to toss the book aside and abandon the undertaking. But persevering and finishing such a book is rewarded with content that expands the reader's world view. In my opinion, this is the true joy of reading. Whereas fiction intended for amusement pleases with narrative and character, the classics enable readers to drink deeply of the joy of coming into direct contact with great writers of the past, of speaking with them and sharing their thoughts.

Since I have read only a small number of them, my interest in the classics will continue for a long time yet. My hope is that I can go on learning from, mentally sharing with, and communing with the geniuses of past ages as I savor their works that have stood the test of time.

## Nichiren: Warmth and Determination

In the twelfth and the thirteenth centuries appeared several great religious leaders who had tremendous impact on the history of Japanese Buddhism. Among them were Shinran (1173–1262), founder of the True Pure Land sect; Dogen (1200–1253), founder of the Soto Zen sect; and Nichiren (1222–82), founder of the Nichiren sect. Other major religious figures of that time include Honen (1133–1212), founder of the Pure Land sect; Eisai (1141–1215), founder of the Rinzai Zen sect; and Ippen (1239–89), founder of the Ji sect of Pure Land Buddhism. Examining the history of Japanese Buddhism, I have become deeply aware of the odd relation between the nature of this historical period and the births of so many religious giants in the space of just a single century.

Theirs was an age of transition, witnessing the dying of the old political order and the rise to authority of the warrior class. The spirit of this era of change—the force behind political and economic power—helped these leaders establish their new schools of Buddhism.

Though contemporaries, Shinran, Dogen, and Nichiren taught very different doctrines. For instance, Shinran believed in the power of the vow of the Buddha Amida, or Amitabha, to save everyone who invokes his name, enabling them to be reborn in his Western Paradise. Dogen, on the other hand, insisted that the way of discipline and self-improve-

## Nichiren

ment is endless and that the active practice of Buddhist discipline is identical with enlightenment.

These three men evolved their own philosophies, refined them, and contributed to the spiritual and social salvation of their time—Nichiren, by far the youngest, as much as the others. More than his nature as a religious reformer, it is the sound, wholesome psychological attitude permeating his entire life that attracts me to Nichiren.

The new values of an age in which the old order was passing and Japan's version of feudalism was coming into being, together with the pessimism that always accompanies a period of transition, colored the thinking of Nichiren's time. In such an age, Nichiren's wholesome approach to life was more welcome than ever because it dispelled the anxiety and distrust lurking in virtually all minds. In our own day, when Japan enjoys a democratic governmental system and material well-being undreamed of a few decades ago, people are insecure and seek something to fill the emptiness of their lives. A similar longing was very strong in Nichiren's day, and he was seen as providing an answer to the prayers of many people.

Although Nichiren was magnanimous and self-confident and had a bright personality, his vigorous denunciation of the Pure Land sects as hellish, of Zen as devilish, of the Shingon sect as ruinous for the whole nation, and of the Ritsu sect as treasonous have earned him a reputation for obstinacy and harshness. But such an assessment overlooks the good sense and kindness that permeate his thinking and attitudes.

Disliking degeneration of any kind, Nichiren was unceasingly eager for progress and development. This is what enabled him to be influential in saving the people of his day from the insecurity and distrust they experienced as part of the prevailing pessimism. His desire for progress led him to exhort government leaders to change their way of thinking and to devote themselves to the teachings of the Lotus Sutra.

But my greatest respect is evoked not so much by Nichiren's lofty contributions to the history of Japanese Buddhism as by his deep and overflowing human warmth, reflected in the many letters of congratulations, thanks, and commiseration he wrote, often to people who are otherwise unknown to history. In one letter he thanks someone for sakè as delicious as nectar; in another he expresses gratitude for dumplings as lovely as the full moon. No doubt these gifts of sakè and dumplings were heartfelt expressions of gratitude from people who visited Nichiren's hermitage to discuss their problems and receive his instruction and advice. He invariably wrote a letter to each person, with thanks for the remembrance.

Nichiren was a religious leader who lived always among ordinary people. There is no denying the force of his individuality, but I think we must remember that his dynamism was coupled with a warm humanity and a spirit of naiveté. He indicated his feelings on filial piety by spending most of his last years on Mount Minobu, southwest of Tokyo, at Shishin-kaku, a temple dedicated to his parents' memory. To a friend who had just celebrated the birth of a child, he wrote a letter in which he said the event was "like flowers blooming in the spring fields." To another who was suffering the loss of a child, he wrote to say he understood the parent's sorrow at a death that was like the premature falling of a young bud.

In my opinion, we get a better understanding of the true personality of Nichiren from letters of this kind than from his more learned and serious dissertations, such as *Kaimoku-sho* (a treatise designed to open the eyes of the unenlightened to the true nature of the Buddha) and *Kanjin Honzon-sho* (a work in which the nature of the true object of religious veneration is set forth).

The contrast between Nichiren's vigorous criticism of religious sects he believed to be wrong and his kindness and consideration for others reminds me of a similar contrast in the personality of Martin Luther, who defied the papacy and became the founder of the Protestant Reformation. History has tended to concentrate on Luther's theological disputes and to overlook the warmth and humanity of his personality, which find expression in the many hymns he wrote in his later years.

In both men, profound humanity was the foundation of a powerful spirit unwilling to flinch no matter what it faced. Furthermore, it was true patriotism and compassion for the society of their times that inspired Nichiren to criticize other Buddhist sects and Luther to undertake the task of religious reformation.

Nichiren may have been a greater patriot than any other hero in Japanese history; yet his approach was not narrow and nationalistic but universal. This is reflected in the passage in *Senji-sho* (a work in which he declares the imperative need to disseminate the Buddhist teachings) to the effect that people may physically do the bidding of their political ruler but must never allow their minds to be subservient to authority. It required not only courage, but also a deep understanding of the human condition to make a bold statement of this kind under the political conditions of his day. These are precisely the things I most admire in Nichiren, who as a youth lived as a novice on Mount Kiyosumi, near his birthplace across the bay from Tokyo, and vowed to become the greatest sage in the nation. In addition, I love the human warmth underlying his stubborn determination and his earnest search for the truth.

## *Emulating Dogen*

Some years ago I had an opportunity to visit the temple Eihei-ji, in Fukui Prefecture, headquarters of the Soto sect of Zen. Because my schedule was very full, I was too pressed for time to make leisurely observations; but as I ate the vegetarian noonday meal, I was strongly impressed by the shaven-headed young priests in somber black robes, who live and train in devotion to Buddhism.

Some engaged in zazen, or seated meditation; others sweated carrying out laborious chores; but completely composed, all of them strictly observed the Buddhist precepts. I noted a large spiritual gap

## Emulating Dogen

between them and ordinary young people, who do exactly as they like but have no purpose. Because the lives of these young priests are totally purposeful, I am convinced that the spirit of the Zen priest Dogen (1200–1253), who founded Eihei-ji, is vibrantly alive there today.

Together with Nichiren, Dogen is one of the figures in Japanese Buddhist history most deserving of respect. At the age of twenty-three—the same age as many of the young priests I saw training at Eihei-ji—Dogen traveled to China to study at the temple Ching-te-ssu, where Eisai (1141–1215), founder of the Rinzai Zen sect, had studied. In later years, reflecting on his trip, Dogen said that all he had learned in China was enlightenment to the truth that his nose was set vertically in the middle of his face and his eyes horizontally on either side of it (that is, to understand ordinary things as ordinary things) and that he had returned home empty-handed, without high-sounding souvenirs like Buddhism.

The kind of training that enabled Dogen to achieve this enlightenment is true discipline, because it is difficult to judge the things of the world with an unclouded eye and to accept the ordinary as ordinary. Another priest would probably have been proud to relate what he had seen and heard in China. But Dogen's casual dismissal of the whole trip as the discovery of his own nose and eyes represents the modest attitude of a great religious leader. Indeed, I entertain the highest respect for him because of the awe-inspiring dignity combined with warm familiarity clearly reflected in his monumental *Shobo-genzo* (Eye Storehouse of the True Law) and in the *Shobo-genzo Zuimonki*, a collection of Dogen's sayings compiled by his disciple Ejo (1198–1280).

The opening section of the *Shobo-genzo* contains the famous statement that from the Buddhist standpoint, if not in the views of non-Buddhist religions, practice and enlightenment are one. Dogen goes on to say that enlightenment is always found in practice and that even the beginner's training practices contain the whole of enlightenment. One cannot expect to find enlightenment outside such practice.

In conclusion, he says that enlightenment that is direct is limitless, since it does not exist outside of practice and self-training. And if enlightenment is found in practice, practice is conducted within enlightenment, as is revealed by the practice of Shakyamuni Buddha, his disciple Maha-Kashyapa, the great Chinese patriarch Bodhidharma, and other great Zen priests throughout the ages. It is because sages like these have practiced discipline within enlightenment that the true Law has been handed down from generation to generation.

In saying that practice and enlightenment are one, Dogen reveals both an all-encompassing purpose for living (enlightenment) and the process whereby that purpose can be achieved (training and practice). All of us give significance to our acts by orienting them toward a goal of some kind. But we should prize the sustained effort necessary to reach a goal more than we prize the goal itself. Once a goal is reached, it ceases to be.

People often talk of living a fulfilled and mean-

## Emulating Dogen

ingful life. A truly meaningful life consists in nothing less than continuing efforts toward goals, rather than evolving perfection in the goals themselves.

The concept of the unity of practice and enlightenment is one of the things I find extremely attractive about the teachings of Dogen. Another is the teaching that kind words have the power to move the heavens. He instructs us to speak to all people outside our family circles with the same warmth and affection we would use in addressing our own children. This means praising the virtues of those who have them and showing compassion to those who do not.

Kind words arise from a kind heart, which is a manifestation of the Buddha's great heart of compassion, which is in turn the source of a desire to bring harmony to all things and happiness to all people. We are able to speak kind words because this desire is at work in our minds all of the time. And when this desire fills the entire world, it will certainly have the power to move the heavens.

A zealous man, Dogen taught that studying Buddhism entails studying oneself and that this means forgetting oneself. He described this state with a phrase signifying perfect freedom of mind and body from all attachments. Human beings usually give precedence to protecting their own being. But this misplaced emphasis confuses and causes contradictions, sufferings, and insecurities. This is why Dogen teaches us to attain lightness and freedom by constantly training to forget ourselves. This is a teaching entirely in keeping with the nature of a person of great zeal who was instrumental in the development of Zen Buddhism in Japan.

One final anecdote gives an excellent idea of Dogen's personality. A priest once said to him: "I am too ill and weak to survive Buddhist practice. Therefore, I should like to hear the most important parts of the Buddhist Law. Then I will separate myself from my family and, living in seclusion, take care of myself for the rest of my life."

In a quiet voice, Dogen replied: "Not all the great religious founders of the past were physically strong. Not all those who diligently trained themselves in the Buddha Way were outstandingly well qualified. Even while Shakyamuni was alive, some trainees faltered. Some of them were of very low caliber. But none of them wept and chose an inferior path for themselves the way you do. If you are lethargic in study and training in this life, no matter how many times you are reborn, it will never be in a superior, healthy form. Apply yourself diligently to study and training for the sake of enlightenment and give no thought to your own illness or survival. This is the way to lead a perfect life."

Whenever I am inclined to be lazy, I recall this incident and try to come closer, if only by one step, to Dogen's way of living. If I ever have the chance, I would like to return to Eihei-ji and join in training with the young priests there who have inherited the robe and alms bowl of this great Zen priest.

## Morning

With its flaming ball of sun, symbolizing the will of the Japanese people, against a pure white background, the Japanese national flag is a most succinct representation of the nation's image. I have the greatest respect for the perspicacity of those people who, in 1870, selected this flag, which had formerly been used as a naval ensign, to represent the Japanese nation. Some of the impressions it awakens in my mind are freshness, devotion, solemnity, eternity, unity, peace, and hope. Perhaps it is part of the aftermath of war that this flag, redolent of such bright connotations, is seen as a nationalistic symbol by some young Japanese. But the time has come for the Japanese to stop looking over their shoulders toward the past and to reevaluate the flag as a representation of the feelings and aspirations of a whole people.

Unaware of lands beyond the vast ocean to the east, unaware even that the earth is a globe, the ancient Japanese believed they were the first to greet the sun each day and proudly called their country the Land of the Rising Sun. Prince-Regent Shotoku (574–622) wrote to Emperor Yang Ti of the Chinese Sui dynasty, sending greetings from the Son of Heaven in the Land Where the Sun Rises to the Son of Heaven in the Land Where the Sun Sets, indicating that in his day the Japanese people were unwilling to bow before even so great a power as China. Today, all this has changed.

The time has come when the Japanese must stop

being concerned with themselves alone and must take a leading role in the effort to unite the peoples of the world, sharing their abundance and happiness. Their mission is to be true to their flag by shedding as much light as they can on the rest of the world.

On another plane, seeing the Japanese flag fluttering in the wind arouses in me associations of morning and the vast, eternal freshness of the world of nature as the sun bursts from behind rosy clouds at dawn. The poet Aritsune Uematsu (1833–1906) is correct when he says: "Nothing is as refreshing as a mind turned toward the morning sun."

How much brighter and happier our whole world would be if all people could carry this morning freshness with them throughout each day! The first day of January is the seed of a whole year; each morning is the seed of a whole day. But many people overlook the importance of morning. It is difficult for urbanites living in sunless streets amid high-rise towers under smog-shrouded skies to catch a glimpse of the sun rising from behind mountains. And the situation is aggravated by the way of life of city-dwelling automatons, who sleep till the last minute, dash some water on their faces, snatch a bite of breakfast, hastily get their things together, and commute to work on crowded trains.

Emperor T'ang of the Yin dynasty, in the seventeenth century B.C., is said to have had engraved on his washing basin the admonition to face each day as something totally new. Although this Chinese emperor no doubt had mainly politics in mind, we could all take a lesson from his approach. We can

## Morning

make each day fuller by getting up ten or twelve minutes earlier than usual, taking advantage of the new day—even if the sky is dimmed by smog—and reflecting on life and the way we should live it.

Introducing the mood of morning into the world of politics would undoubtedly benefit it as well. In the distant past, when the scale of Japan's government was small, ministers gathered at court early in the morning to confer with the monarch, to discuss and plan the day's affairs. It is now common for the Diet to confer late into the night, and I cannot help thinking this has had a baleful effect on political behavior. Perhaps things in general would take a turn for the brighter if the Diet started meeting at daybreak, an hour consonant with the ideals of a nation symbolized by the rising sun.

Whenever I travel, I always look forward with greatest pleasure to those unexpected sunrises I have a chance to view. And as the solar orb rises beyond the horizon or emerges from ranges of mountains, I automatically bring my hands together in prayer that for that day I will be able to live strongly and unflinchingly. Having something for which to live requires not revolutionary or idealistic goals but the will to rise and face a new day, eager to live freely and to fight the battles of life courageously. The whole world would progress toward a better future if this attitude became the foundation of our thoughts and acts.

Many of the people who claim to have lost all reason to live have actually done nothing of the kind. They have simply allowed themselves to become so shortsighted and so entangled with transitory things that they can do nothing but chafe, complain, and criticize. Declaring that one has nothing to live for is tantamount to rejecting one's value as a human being. People who do this are too jaded to be moved either by the red ball of the sun on a flag or even by the glorious rising sun itself ushering in a new day.

Yet such feelings can be changed by the mood of morning, by hope and awe in the face of the eternal, and by the devotion that the morning mood inspires. It is time to abandon trivialities and to reinvigorate our minds and hearts with the freshness and humility born of daybreak.

*Seasonal Reflections*

## *The Bush Warbler*

In the congested city in which I live, the song of the bush warbler still announces the arrival of spring each year. My mother, whose ear is keen, narrows her eyes in pleasure as she gazes into the garden and says: "I heard the first bush warbler today. It's come again this year."

I rise too late to hear the bird in the early morning and usually hear it in the garden two or three days after Mother has already made her announcement. Nonetheless, the bird's message that even in the urban asphalt jungle the seasons keep their appointed rounds brings joy to my heart. Tree branches, their buds closed tight against the cold, rattle beneath gray skies and hint of the brightness and warmth soon to come. I recall a song we sang when I was a primary school pupil in the snowy mountains of Niigata Prefecture: "In the eastern wind of the mountains in March I can hear the sounds of spring."

The song is redolent of many things associated

with my childhood, all of which rush back to me every time I hear it. If I had been raised in the city, I doubt that the song would have impressed me as strongly as it has. For me, a man raised in a part of the country where the winters are long and severe, nothing means spring so much as that song and the melody of the bush warbler.

Humming the tune to myself, eyes closed, I can see the village where we lived. In March our mountain home is still blanketed deep in snow. The cold winds howl down the slopes to the icy, snow-packed road we walk to school, singing that children's song, our hearts filled with the hope that spring will come soon. Then the snow begins to melt, releasing the frozen streams and sending them murmuring on their way. The tops of the raised paths among the fields turn muddy, and the soil of the paddy plots begins appearing as black patches in the lingering white. A brighter sun warms our backs and shoulders and gently caresses our frost-bitten fingers. Surely there can never have been a sun as brimming with brilliance as this one. No longer does the harsh north wind set branches clacking against each other. In its place, the gentle eastern wind—the eastern wind of the song—blows with such kindness that, straining to hear it, we children consider its very touch a wonderful gift.

I doubt that people of my age who were raised in the city were able to enjoy the simple happiness the arrival of spring gave to us in the country. And since my childhood the urban environment has changed and been separated from the ordinary cycle of nature to become a jungle of elevated highways, traffic jams, and reinforced-concrete buildings.

Perhaps there is nothing to be done about the urban environment, but it is regrettable that as the world of nature grows more and more remote, relations among urbanites become increasingly tenuous. Awareness of the passing of the seasons—as the earth is covered with snow, as the trees burst into flower, as evening showers wash the trees, and as gold and red autumn leaves dance downward foretelling the end of another year—colors every day and enriches human emotional life. The absence of this awareness makes human beings insensitive, creates thorny relations between them, and coarsens their thoughts and actions. In spite of all that, however, people speak rashly of conquering nature, in the shallow belief that that is the way to build a better society.

We are born in the world of nature, and it is by means of the world of nature that we are able to live. How can we think of conquering nature, without which we cannot survive?

The poets in the magnificent eighth-century anthology *Man'yoshu* were able to write gems like "The bud of bracken droops above the boulder-bound stream, telling of spring" because their hearts were filled with understanding of nature and because they knew the deep longing for verdure and warmth that comes at the end of a long winter. When I look at arid cities in which warped human beings crowd, I become homesick for the springs I knew as a child in the mountains. That is why I hope the bush warbler will always bring its melodious, vernal song to the garden of my urban home.

## Crossing to the Opposite Shore

In Buddhist terms, the world into which we are born is called "this shore"; the realm of Nirvana is called "the opposite shore" (*higan* in Japanese). In Japan the weeks of the spring and autumnal equinoxes (*higan* in Japanese), during which people visit cemeteries to remember the dead, are observed in a way that strikes me as both tender and distinctively oriental.

A few years ago I visited India and walked the banks of the Ganges, which flows just as it did twenty-five hundred years ago, in Shakyamuni's time. The sight of the river's immense breadth gave me a renewed understanding of why Shakyamuni likened attaining Nirvana to crossing to the opposite shore. It may be that the *higan* philosophy did not originate in Japan, since none of Japan's rivers is comparable in width to the Ganges. I was disturbed to think that the Japanese have tended to emphasize the ritual nature of *higan* while overlooking its essential meaning.

People today generally lack interest in ideals like that of the opposite shore. Some fret only about what happens on this shore. Others live their days in tranquillity, giving no thought to ideals of any kind. I am saddened to see that our society has no interest in striving for higher goals or in making the world we live in a little better and brighter.

Shakyamuni Buddha taught us to strive diligently to reach the other shore, even though we must live in the uncleanness of this one. Individuals, families, groups, and society at large must endeavor to achieve the same thing. While remembering lost loved ones and praying for their repose during the weeks of the spring and autumnal equinoxes, we should give thought to living in a way that will enable us all to reach the opposite shore of tranquillity and peace.

## Cherry Blossoms

Beyond our fence, in our neighbor's yard, are two large cherry trees that delight our eyes every spring with masses of blossoms, right in the heart of Tokyo. I have developed a real affection for those trees. As I sit by my open window watching their pale pink blossoms dance in the breeze, I recall a perfectly apt poem from the *Kokinshu*, an anthology of poems in the *waka* style completed in 905:

> In spite of the spring day's tender sun,
> Uneasily the cherry blossoms fall.

The flavor of the verse cannot be savored, however, in the clamor and drinking of the usual cherry-blossom-viewing party; it demands quiet and solitude, which in our day and time are great luxuries.

But the very joy of seeing the cherry blossoms is undermined by the fear of a sudden wind that will tear them from their boughs. When I hear night winds blowing in the cherry-blossom season, I am especially concerned for the welfare of the blossoms on our neighbor's trees. The Chinese poet Meng Hao-jan (689–740) wrote:

> Sleeping in spring, oblivious of daybreak,
> I hear the birds singing.
> Last night I heard the sounds of wind and rain.
> How many blossoms fell, I wonder.

Although I am not sure what kind of blossom the poet had in mind, he was concerned about them, as I am about the cherry blossoms.

I do not suggest that cherry trees are beautiful only when in full bloom. There is splendor when the blossoms fall, too. People of the past compared the glory of the blossoms in their last moment on the branch to that of a courageous samurai in constant danger of being cut down in his prime. Unlike other flowers, the cherry blossom does not wither before it falls. When I catch one in the palm of my hand, I am overcome with pity and the idea that somehow it can be returned to the bough.

But our part of town, where we can still see our neighbor's cherry trees, is changing. Not long ago an unsightly telephone pole was erected next to one of the trees. At night fluorescent street lamps now prevent viewing the cherry blossoms by the light of a partly cloud-concealed moon, a pleasure described by a seventeenth-century Japanese poet whose name I cannot recall:

> Clouds come for the sake of the moon,
> Winds for the sake of the blooms.

> Because of clouds and winds,
> Moon and blooms are more precious.

Perhaps I should resign myself to being deprived of such feelings in the bustle and clamor of the modern world.

## Flowers of Kyoto

With today's bullet trains traveling from Tokyo to Kyoto in just a few hours, a trip to the ancient capital when the cherry trees are in bloom—which I had long wanted to make—is simplicity itself, especially by comparison with the journey people of past centuries had to make on foot over the fifty-three stages of the old Tokaido highway. Nonetheless, because of the many functions I must attend in that season, it was many years before I found time to travel to Kyoto in the spring.

I had only three days and two nights free, but I thought even that brief period would be enough to let me savor the ambiance of a sea of cherry blossoms in the heart of Japan's traditional culture. All I actually saw, however, was people, people, and more people. The restful stay I had hoped for turned out to be more hectic than my ordinary daily life.

We arrived at noon. Without stopping to change clothes, I set out immediately to see the Shisen-do and Nijo Castle. The Shisen-do is the hermitage of Ishikawa Jozan (1583–1672), a warrior who became a Buddhist priest and a renowned scholar. It is located in spacious, beautifully kept grounds and suggests the elegance and dignity one would expect of a residence that a man of letters built for his final years. The name Shisen-do, or Hall of the Immortal Poets, derives from the paintings of thirty-six great Chinese poets adorning the walls of one of its rooms. I found the garden with its budding greenery more appealing than the room from which I viewed it. At Nijo Castle, although that was my second visit, I was unprepared for the breathtaking splendor of its gardens when the cherry trees were in full bloom.

On the following day, a Saturday, the city was more congested than before. Unable to find a taxi, I rented a car to go to the temples Ninna-ji, Tenryu-ji, and Saiho-ji, and to Mount Hiei. My impression of the day was that people were more conspicuous than cherry blossoms. Only at Ninna-ji was the crowd small enough to allow me to enjoy some of the beauty of spring in Kyoto. One of the best parts of the day was when I enjoyed a steaming bowl of tofu at a restaurant near Tenryu-ji.

On the third day, I again went sightseeing among the crowds. Since I had to return to Tokyo in the afternoon, I had planned to rely on taxis that day. It was irritating to have to waste a great deal of time before finally managing to find one. By then I had just enough time for hurried looks at the temple Kiyomizu-dera and the Heian Shrine.

I was disappointed to realize that my long-cherished hopes for the trip had been too high. Perhaps it is impossible nowadays to enjoy leisurely strolls at historic places, beneath boughs of cherry trees in bloom.

## The Northeast

As our train glided out of the canyons of Tokyo's tall buildings on my first trip to the Tohoku, a region far to the northeast of Tokyo, brilliant green foliage rustled in the wind and flashed in the sunlight till my eyes seemed to be cleansed by the very sight. Thoughts of such poets as Basho, Takuboku, Bansui Doi, and Kenji Miyazawa inspired me to vow to write a haiku about my trip.

After reaching Sendai, we set out in the afternoon for the famous island-studded Matsushima Bay, which is considered one of the most beautiful scenic attractions in Japan. But I was disheartened to find that the sea there is now as polluted as Tokyo Bay.

On the following day we went to Hiraizumi to see the temple Chuson-ji. As chance would have it, however, ceremonies were being held to celebrate the completion of the restoration of the temple's famous Konjiki-do, or Golden Hall. The temple so overflowed with tourists that it was impossible to stroll through its grounds or to talk with local people about the first three generations of the Fujiwara family—who, beginning in the eleventh century, were responsible for a brilliant cultural flowering in that part of the country and whose mummified bodies are kept at Chuson-ji.

After the disappointments of Matsushima and Hiraizumi, my expectations for the Tohoku region were fading until, at Hananomaki, I had the opportunity to meet and talk with the younger brother of the late poet Kenji Miyazawa.

I wondered at the strangeness of human emotions when, as a consequence of that meeting, my chagrin vanished. It made the whole journey worthwhile. Our conversation deeply impressed me with Kenji's modesty and the religious faith that imbued his life. His brother's final words to me were about the way Kenji revealed his faith from within himself without attempting to teach or expound it. Throughout his humble life, Kenji was a man filled with the kind of inner faith that—as the great Japanese Buddhist priest Saicho (767–822) said—is the mainstay of a seeker of the Way, brightening the corner where it is found.

On my third day in the Tohoku region, I visited the city of Morioka, famous as the birthplace of the respected early twentieth-century prime minister Takashi Hara. The Tohoku region's vast spaces struck me as suitable for the cultivation of Hara and other men like him who made great contributions to the development of Japan as a modern state. This trip to the northeast deeply impressed me with the importance of nature—mountains, rivers, and beautiful human relations—in our environment.

On the homeward train, I realized that I had neglected the haiku I had intended to write. Basho was able to write one splendid poem after another on his trips, but I was incapable of even one. Finally resolving to produce something and turning to look out the window for inspiration, I found we were already racing through the neon-lit outskirts of Tokyo. I consoled myself that the writing of poetry should be left to gifted observers like Basho and Takuboku: any haiku of mine could only contribute to the further destruction of the Tohoku scenery.

## Late-spring Verdure

Is there any season that makes a person feel so glad to be alive as late spring, especially in May, when the sun beams down on fresh, new green leaves glittering in the breeze? On late-spring days I find it impossible to remain still.

In Japan one of the most beautiful sights of May is carp streamers (*koinobori*), which seem to swim bravely in the late-spring sky. I can only wonder what genius devised this beautiful object that suits the season so handsomely.

Reference books say that the carp is a folk symbol for a messenger who summons the gods and that the practice of making sleevelike cloth banners colorfully painted to look like carp and flying them in celebration of the traditional boys' festival on May 5 originated around the middle of the Edo period (1603–1868). The vigor of the carp, long regarded as a symbol of success, is somehow transferred to the banners, which seem to struggle against the current in an ever-upward swim.

By the middle of the Edo period, the burgeoning

culture of the newly emerging merchant and artisan class was supporting a lively creativity that saw nothing incongruous in comparing the sky to cascading water. The *koinobori* is an example of the art that evolved from the daily lives of these people.

Full sets of *koinobori,* consisting of several large carp-shaped streamers, are growing so rare in crowded modern cities that if I come upon one while out walking, I have to stop and gaze, forgetful of time.

I imagine that all Japanese share my belief that these carp banners rank high among the world's many beautiful things. I say this because a televison report I saw on Japanese residing abroad showed them looking up happily at *koinobori* flying against a background of ancient European castles. *Koinobori* in distant lands bring happiness and thoughts of home to Japanese. The sight filled me with gratitude for the aesthetic sensibilities of our ancestors who created these beautiful banners.

In addition to the lovely sight of *koinobori,* May and its new greenery bring feelings of good health accompanied by optimism and strength. When I see the sky and the verdure that speak of the vigor of the season, I always recall the words of the New Testament: "Do not be anxious, saying, 'What shall we eat?' or 'What shall we drink?' or 'What shall we wear?' . . . Your heavenly Father knows that you need them all. But seek first his kingdom and all his righteousness, and all these things shall be yours as well. Therefore do not be anxious about tomorrow,

## Late-spring Verdure

for tomorrow will be anxious for itself. Let the day's own trouble be sufficient for the day" (Matthew 6:31–34).

Though modern people who cannot live without taking thought of tomorrow may find this an extremely optimistic piece of advice, I think it sets forth the way we ought to live. Of course it is important to think about the future, but worrying so much about what lies ahead that the present is filled with anxiety can scarcely be called a progressive approach. More than anything else, people need to cultivate the psychological latitude and relaxation to live each day as fully as possible.

Viewed in perspective, this *carpe diem* philosophy reflects the way of life of Buddhist leaders of the past who trained themselves diligently to make spiritual progress while living day by day on the food that they received as mendicants. Throughout their lives, these great sages followed the Way unwaveringly and, like the birds of the air and the lilies of the field mentioned in the Sermon on the Mount, lived each day in simplicity and humility.

If the words "heavenly Father" are replaced with the word "Buddha," it becomes apparent that the message in the passage I quoted from the Bible is consonant with the spirit of Buddhism. It is often said that East is East and West is West, but the ideals and the optimum way of life for which all human beings strive are the same everywhere. We can all learn a great deal from teachings that advocate an optimistic, wholesome way of life.

## *Summer Thoughts*

Sounds of summer bring back memories of the heat of the season when I was a small boy. I vividly recall traveling for a long time on a packed train in 1944, when we were evacuated to my parents' childhood home in Niigata Prefecture to escape the danger of war. My child's mind could barely accept the broiling heat with which the country fields and mountains greeted us when we finally arrived.

A Tokyo-bred child, I knew I had traveled far from everything familiar when I sniffed the sour stench that flowed into the entranceway of our house from the adjacent stable. It is usual to associate heavy snowfalls with Niigata, but probably because I was so struck by our new way of life there, at the mention of Niigata I still recall the indelible impressions of that first hot day.

Oddly, however, my recollections of summer in the country stop there and do not begin again until my fifth or sixth year of primary school. I must have heard the emperor's radio broadcast in August 1945 announcing Japan's surrender, but I cannot remember it or what I was doing or saying at the time.

For a short while after our arrival, the local children treated us as outsiders, city slickers. As well as the heat, I remember that until we were accepted my sisters and I played marbles by ourselves in a corner of the schoolyard.

But it was not long before we were splashing and swimming with new friends in the pond in front of the school—the same pond where we picked pink or white lotus flowers to take home to offer at the family Buddhist altar as part of the celebration of the midsummer Bon festival, during which ancestral spirits are believed to visit their families. We knew at last the long-awaited festival had come when we saw the lotus flowers in the flickering golden glow of candle-lit lanterns.

In the evening air, the deep, vaguely inviting sound of a drum echoed in the forest surrounding the village tutelary Shinto shrine. Then, as the sweet tones of a flute rippled over the paddy fields, everyone in the village gradually assembled in the shrine precincts, where they formed circles and, to the accompaniment of festive music, danced the Bon festival folk dances late into the night, forgetful of everything else.

In those days the Bon festival was practically the only entertainment village people had, and everyone looked forward eagerly to the chance it gave them to forget a whole year's hardships in one evening of dancing and talking. Just after the war, when I was there, food was scarce and there was none of the feasting enjoyed now. And though our holiday clothes were the carefully-cared-for best we had, they were coarse and poor. Life was hard but no one complained. Instead they endured bravely, sharing what little pleasure and joy came their way and helping each other as much as possible.

When I look back, I cannot help feeling that those country people knew the way human beings ought to live. It makes me sad to see that now, some decades later, the simple pleasures we knew then have been forgotten and everything centers on money. Reflecting on this inspires even greater respect for the way people of the past knew how to discover joy in a simple life. As Confucius says in the *Analects:* "Simple food to eat, water to drink, and my own arm for a pillow: pleasure is found in these."

Those are some summer-related recollections of my distant past. The hot weather brings back another, more recent. Some years ago I climbed Mount Fuji. Though mountains are green and refreshing seen from afar, on close inspection they all turn out to be stony, steep, and covered with briars and brambles. Even worse, they are often sullied with trash left behind by human beings. Consequently, I long ago resolved to view Mount Fuji's peerlessly graceful form only from a distance and never to climb that mountain, especially since people had told me of the heaps of discarded cans and other trash littering its slopes all the way to the summit, evidence of human intrusion inconsonant with the mountain's fame as a holy place.

But pressing reasons led me to violate my resolve, and the minute I had started climbing Mount Fuji I realized that all the bad things I had heard were true. Trash was everywhere. Even more surprising to me were the harsh cinders and lava of slopes that looked so blue and lovely from a distance. The reality of Mount Fuji and my idealized image of it were worlds apart. My image gradually crumbled with the crunching sounds my feet made as I climbed upward.

That experience deeply impressed me with the

validity of the truism that reality and the ideal rarely coincide. This applies to human relations too. I experienced terrible disillusionment after encountering the true nature of a person I had from childhood idealized as a paragon of virtue. Confronted with the real person, my idealized image faded, leaving me in despair.

The lesson from that kind of experience is that we should keep our eyes open to reality as we pursue our ideals, and always test our ideals against reality. Refusal to look at reality prevents our understanding the true nature of things; refusal to look at anything *but* reality leads to despair and does not inspire spiritual growth. As I climbed Mount Fuji that hot summer day, I kept telling myself that harmony between the ideal and the real is the goal to strive for.

## The Oze Highlands

I had long wanted to visit the Oze Highlands, which stretch across the juncture of Gumma, Niigata, and Fukushima prefectures. When I arrived in that nature preserve, I was immediately struck with the freshness of everything and with a feeling that I was regaining something I had lost years earlier. Still, my guide, who had been there often, was disappointed to see that the celebrated highland *mizubasho*, or skunk cabbage, which blooms in the cold waters of highland marshes and has a white flower resembling the calla lily, had passed its peak and that it no longer bloomed in places where it had once been abundant. "Oze is being ruined more and more every year," he said with a sigh. His comment came as a surprise to a person like me, who had found everything, including the *mizubasho*, extremely lovely.

As a city dweller who has little contact with unspoiled nature, I never stopped exclaiming in wonder at the flowers and the cool winds blowing across the highlands.

That night we slept in a crude mountain lodge. Since electricity was supplied by the lodge's own small generator, the lights were turned out at eight, when we were expected to go to sleep. For city people things are just beginning at eight o'clock. Nonetheless, we climbed into our beds and, unable to sleep, chatted until eight-thirty, when the generator stopped and everything went black and silent.

Enjoying the dark silence and the cold highland air, I recalled thoughts I had had in earlier years about nature and civilization: it is wrong for civilized life to be as divorced from the world of nature as it is; living in nature, human beings must obey natural laws by at least going to bed at sunset and getting up at sunrise; relying on electricity and staying up till all hours of the night violate natural laws. Later I came to feel that these thoughts were too juvenile to reveal and decided to keep them to myself. But that night at Oze, forced to go to bed early because of nature's primacy, I came to suspect that perhaps my reflections had not entirely missed the mark.

Though my view is open to criticism as extreme,

## The Oze Highlands

there is no question that while reaping many benefits from modern civilization, we have moved farther away from nature, with which our ties become increasingly more tenuous. As I lay in the dark that night, I asked myself if such a lifestyle can lead to true happiness. Some people accept the rapid development of our society as being essential to happiness. Yet, is it wise to ignore nature?

With such thoughts running through my mind, before I knew it I had fallen asleep. The next morning I awoke to a virtual concert of bush warblers, cuckoos, and many other kinds of birds. I captured some of their music with the portable tape recorder I had taken along. I recorded still more birdsong as we made our way through the trees to visit the Sanjo waterfall.

As we walked I suddenly recalled a poem I once read—unfortunately I do not remember the author's name:

> Going to the mountains,
> What did I do?
> Going to the mountains,
> I walked crunching
> And drank some water.

At Oze the verse had a meaning different from when I read it at my desk. Unpretentious, unadorned poetry of this kind, probably an emotional response jotted down as the poet walked through scenery of the kind we were enjoying that day, always has a fresh appeal that transcends time and place.

After we stood awhile, wiping sweat from our

faces and gazing at the splendid Sanjo waterfall, which is compared for majesty with Kegon Falls at Nikko, we returned to the lodge for our backpacks. We then hiked past Mount Shibutsu and across the Oze Plain. The countless wildflowers covering the plain kept it from being monotonous by comparison with the scenery in the mountains.

Far from the pollution of the big city, turning my ear to the murmuring of streams, the calls of birds, and the gentle rustling of leaves, I felt as if I were inside a picture or a poem.

Then suddenly the sky grew overcast and rain fell. But it was welcome rain. I was grateful for the varied panorama of the mountains, enjoyed now in soft sunlight, now in gentle wind, and now in drenching rain.

## *Evening Showers*

After the hot summer sun has blazed all day, sometimes the late-afternoon sky suddenly goes dark: thunder crashes, and buildings, highways, and people are enveloped in a roaring deluge. For city people it is the most refreshing thing possible. All the dust is washed away from city streets.

When I look through the rain at the swirling rivers carrying away trash carelessly discarded by humanity, I am astonished by the insignificance of cities in comparison with the forces of nature. Intoxicated by our civilization's achievements and prosperity, we tend to forget nature's might until something like a summer-evening squall reminds us. Sudden evening showers seem to me a heaven-sent reminder that the forces of nature affect human beings as much as other forms of life.

The refreshed feeling one enjoys after an evening thunderstorm seems to revive one's humanity. Fond of these brief, heavy rains, I like to sit by an open window, not at all frightened by the thunder and lightning, enjoying the drama mighty nature performs for impotent humanity.

When the cloudburst is over, the blue sky reappears, and cicadas sing in the freshly washed branches of the trees. Cool breezes fan my perspiring skin, and for an instant I feel cleansed to my innermost being.

The other day, after such a rain an immense rainbow—rare over Tokyo—arched across the sky. I hurried for my camera before it could vanish and took pictures of a phenomenon that I enjoyed nearly all the time as a child but that is extraordinary in the big city.

When the photographs were developed they were a pale reflection of the real rainbow. Nonetheless, I was satisfied to have captured a display of nature. And I still take them out from time to time and recall the fresh brilliance of the colors as they really were.

## Winds

Some years ago I discovered how accurate the ninth-century poet and calligrapher Fujiwara no Toshiyuki was in this poetic description:

To my eyes it is not clear that autumn has come,
But the chill whisper of the invisible wind
Startles me into awareness.

One windy day, when a perfectly ordinary rain fell, I hurried to close a window only to discover that rain was not blowing in through it at all. In summer the slightest rain soaks everything near this window if it is left open. Wondering what had changed, I went to the other side of the house and found a closed window covered with rain that would have spoiled the room if the window had been open.

Of course! It was autumn and the winds had shifted direction. The poet knew autumn had arrived when he felt the winds blowing from a quarter other than the one from which they had come all summer.

The wind is a miraculous phenomenon: no one knows whence it comes or whither it goes; no one has ever seen it. It differs according to time and season. The dawn wind that blows hope and seems to offer encouragement for the new day is unlike any other. Many winds are welcome—the cool breeze of a summer night, the refreshing winds blowing down a mountain valley, the nostalgia-laden evening wind that pushes high piles of crimson clouds across an autumn sunset sky. But no one is gladdened by the sharp winds of winter or the gusty, wet blowing of the typhoon. The wind's personalities are as diverse as our reactions to them.

*Fu*, the Japanese word for wind (written with an ideogram read *feng* in Chinese), resembles the

English word *air* in that it can also mean appearance, deportment, manner, or atmosphere. In Japan the general mood of a family or a company is described as its *fu*, or wind.

The Chinese anthology *Shih Ching* (Classic of Poetry), compiled between the eleventh and sixth centuries B.C., uses the word *wind* as a rubric for folk songs from various regions because songs are as invisible as the wind, though both have the power to move us, one emotionally and the other physically. If we employ the ancient Chinese view, the air, or wind, of a family or company too has the power to move others.

Though no one can do anything about nature's wind, we can all work to ensure that our families and the other groups and organizations to which we belong move the minds of our fellow human beings for the better. This thought always crosses my mind when I hear the wind rapping at my door.

## Flying to the Moon

Stepping into the garden, where the insects were chirping, I looked up at the moon and suddenly realized that lunar landings have changed all the ideas people long entertained about the moon. The lunar utopias of early science fiction have evaporated. No longer can the Japanese entertain traditional fancies of a princess of legend living on the moon or of rabbits pounding glutinous-rice cakes on its surface. Epoch-making achievements in human history, lunar landings have destroyed many ancient fancies.

The Apollo astronauts' diaries paint a picture far removed from romance when they describe the moon as bleak and forbidding, devoid of life and of any evidence that life ever existed there. The moon is nothing but an immense mass of pocked, gray pumice.

This knowledge may cripple poets who sing of the beauty of the moon. And many Japanese who formerly observed the custom of viewing the autumn full moon with offerings of dumplings and pampas grass will no doubt change their thinking about the moon's mystical beauty. Personally, I will always think first of humankind's great achievement in space exploration and admire the moon's beauty as an afterthought.

Looking at the moon now makes me deeply aware of living in the space age. In the light of the bold achievements space exploration represents, it is unreasonable of us to lament the loss of our old fancies when we can be fascinated by the astronauts' impressions of earth seen from the moon.

They spoke of observing the royal blue of the oceans, the yellows and browns of the land masses, and the white of clouds. Little more than three and half times the size of the moon, the earth held all hope, all life, everything the astronauts knew and loved. It was the most beautiful thing they could see in the whole universe. These men thought that other people could not comprehend how much they have without leaving the planet and then returning to it.

The astronauts' impressions of earth from the moon reminded me of a passage in chapter 16 of the

Lotus Sutra, "Revelation of the [Eternal] Life of the Tathagata," where the Buddha says: "Tranquil is this realm of mine, / Ever filled with heavenly beings, / Parks, and many palaces / With every kind of gem adorned, / Precious trees full of blossoms and fruits, / Where all creatures take their pleasure."

As is made clear by the astronauts' moving description of earth as seen from the moon and as is pointed out with accuracy and truth in the Buddha's teachings, our earth is the most beautiful thing in the universe. The astronauts' comment that human beings do not realize the worth of all they have is a clear warning to humanity to stop laying waste to the world through pollution and destruction of the natural environment.

Many of us seem to have forgotten how fortunate we are to have been born into this world of jeweled trees where we can live in happiness and pleasure, and we see no need to be grateful for our blessings. Ironically, the opening of the space age shows us how wrong our ingratitude is and teaches us to look down and make a new, more appreciative examination of our earth.

Socrates lived according to the words above the door of the temple of Apollo: "Know thyself." The dawning of the space age brings the import of these words home to us with renewed force.

We must love and glorify the earth, our home, and strive to make it worthy of becoming the Land of Tranquil Light of Shakyamuni Buddha's teachings.

When the astronauts described in detail what

they actually saw on the surface of the moon, their prosaic description angered some poets. The astronauts said the surface of the far side of the moon resembles a dirty beach. This, according to them, is fact, not fancy. It looks like a badly damaged volleyball court on a gray beach.

Those words reminded me of a favorite poem of the Southern Sung dynasty (1127–1279) by Chen Shan-min:

> In the mountains, the moon I love,
> Suspended brightly over a sparse grove,
> Pities a man in deep solitude,
> Shedding its rays on his robe and collar.
> My heart is like the moon, by itself,
> And the moon like my heart.
> My heart and the moon light up one another,
> Conversing far into a clear night.

Now that we know something of the harsh reality of the moon, poetry like this can enrich the beauty of its light.

## The Night Sky

Recently, even on cool autumn evenings the Tokyo sky is so leaden and overcast that we must feel ourselves fortunate to glimpse the occasional star or two. If we recall the charming lyrics we sang as children about the first evening star and descriptions we read of a sky strewn with silver sand, we can only wonder at the vast, magnificent firmament that we trust survives somewhere beyond the smog. We realize im-

# The Night Sky

mediately that our grandest adjectives cannot describe its infinity. The universe is mystical, but human beings, though no more than microscopic particles in the universe, are amazing too in that they contemplate this cosmic mystery.

Light takes an average of about 8.3 minutes to traverse the distance between the sun and the earth and an average of not quite 1.3 seconds to cover that between the moon and the earth. The distances involved in cosmic relations are astoundingly great, but light crosses them with amazing speed. For instance, it can circle the earth almost seven and a half times in just one second. Even traveling at this speed, however, light takes about 2 million years to reach the Andromeda Nebula and about 39 million years to reach the star Virgo A in the constellation Virgo. In comparison with such inconceivable vastness, how very tiny seem all the clamorous problems of our earth.

It is thought that our solar system came into being about 4.7 billion years ago. Primitive bacteria and algae had already developed on earth by about 3.2 billion years ago. From these beginnings evolved all plants and animals, culminating in the appearance of humankind.

In comparison with the history of the solar system, the million or so years humans have been on earth is extremely brief. If we compare the length of the solar system's history to the height of Mount Fuji, the history of the human race would equal far less than a meter, just three or four paces for someone climbing to the summit of that mountain. Incomprehensible as it may seem, we humans—living our daily lives, laughing, weeping, raging, and rejoicing on the planet earth—are as minuscule as poppy seeds in the universal vastness.

Another cause for occasional astonishment is the number of stars in the universe. Scientists say there are over 100 billion in our galaxy alone. The light stars give off is so bright that observers on earth cannot at present detect any planets near them. But if a technique for discovering planets like ours at great distances can be developed, the number of known heavenly bodies in the universe may increase to trillions.

It seems almost certain that life similar to what we know on earth exists on some other planets. Living creatures, perhaps of kinds we cannot imagine, may have created their own distinctive civilizations on those planets. I feel a certain kinship with creatures who, though separated from us by hundreds or even thousands of light years, join us as members of the same universal community.

Humankind, comparatively no larger than a poppy seed, has already pooled intelligence and technical skills to send people to the moon and is now preparing to travel outside the solar system. Advances into outer space will mark a new epoch not only in human history but also in the history of the universe.

On the basis of present data, scientists predict that in perhaps 10 billion years the sun will have lost its energy and expanded to eighty-four times its present size, bringing its surface into Mercury's orbit, burning up the inner planets in the solar system, and putting an end to life on earth. Scientists

# The Night Sky

consider this fate virtually inescapable, and it may be presumptuous of us to think that humankind can survive forever.

Nonetheless, I wonder how human beings will apply their accumulated wisdom when and if the prophesied end comes. Will we tranquilly accept a flaming destiny? Or will we sail forth into the cosmos in search of a new planet? The very idea is profoundly mystical.

In connection with the predicted end of the world, I should like to comment on the kind of fatalism that such a prediction stimulates, especially as a century draws to a close. The realization that the end is approaching can spur people to reexamine their way of living and thinking, or it can lead to despair and the willful destruction of all aspirations and dreams. The second response results only in a pervasive spiritual desolation. For instance, though Halley's comet is seen only briefly about every seventy-six years, in past centuries it has been interpreted as a sign of the end of the world by some people, who then descended to debauchery, demonstrating that despair can end in spiritual ruin.

Some people mistakenly believe that the fundamental Buddhist doctrine that nothing is permanent is a teaching of hopelessness and despair. That is not what Shakyamuni Buddha intended. His purpose in revealing the ephemeral nature of all things was to inspire in us a constant willingness to seek the new. We must not think that the things we see before us are permanent. Even happiness is of uncertain duration. Consequently, instead of wishing for a continuation of the status quo, we must always try to adapt to change by discovering or creating better ways to live. In short, Shakyamuni's teaching that nothing is permanent calls us to be always mentally active and alert and to build the future by means of ceaseless regeneration.

Some aspects of the present world situation, such as the population explosion and the problem of limited natural resources, do seem to foretell disaster. But I feel our knowledge of the full picture is still too limited to allow us to despair. Though we must not ignore them, dry scientific facts alone do not explain everything. The universe is too vast and too filled with possibilities for us to fathom it with our small store of knowledge.

In the great sixteenth-century Chinese comic novel *Hsi-yu chi* (Record of a Journey to the West), a magically gifted monkey runs till he reaches what he thinks is the end of the world and writes his name on a pillar he finds there. Only later does he learn that he has been dashing about in the palm of the Buddha's hand and that what he thought was a pillar is one of the Buddha's fingers.

We are very much like that monkey when we attempt to restrict the infinite, starry universe to fit the facts currently available to us.

## *Life in the Snow Country*

Though I have lived a long time in Tokyo, where snow is rare, to me winter still means dancing snowflakes and a whole world—fields, houses, and forests—concealed in an

## Life in the Snow Country

eaves-high blanket of white. Not even long residence in Tokyo can erase from my mind the images of snow during my years from primary school through senior high school, which I spent in my father's home village of Tokamachi, in Niigata Prefecture.

Light flurries may inspire lyrical ideas of snow-viewing boats gliding down mountain streams, as depicted in traditional Japanese ink paintings. But the snows we knew were freezing blizzards that piled snow so deep that patches remained on the ground even after the spring thaw. Snow reminds me of the need for perseverance to survive the hard life mountain people lead: day in, day out, the same tasks and, it seems, the same snow blowing at you almost horizontally, making it impossible to walk without leaning. Only a person who has lived in the snow country understands how far life there is removed from lyricism.

I remember how I cried because of the extreme cold when we first moved to Niigata to escape the dangers of life in Tokyo during World War II. But since returning to Tokyo I have forgotten all the hardships of my earliest years in Niigata and remember only vignettes demonstrating the warmth of our way of life. For instance, I recall the crunching sound that our huge snowshoes made as we walked the road full of snowdrifts to school, the snowball fights we had after we got there, and the novelty of shoveling snow five or six feet deep from the roof. And of course, most indelible of all are memories of New Year's Eve and New Year's in the snow.

As the Buddhist temple bell sounded out on New Year's Eve, according to custom everyone headed for the local Shinto shrine to make a pilgrimage straddling two years, the outgoing and the incoming. The custom was honored even if a blizzard raged. We merely pulled our straw hats down over our ears or wrapped towels around our heads for protection from the cold as we trudged to the shrine, exchanging seasonal greetings with the fellow villagers we met on our way. In the light reflected from the snow, we appeared a picture of fantasy as, on the way home, we called out wishes for prosperity and happiness in the new year.

Our village shrine was a small, modest affair of about twelve square meters. For New Year's—though at no other time—the floor was covered with woven grass mats. A forty-watt light bulb suspended from the ceiling and two or three flickering candles glowed in front of the sanctuary. The simplicity of the shrine echoed the simplicity of life in the village. But to us children the rustic building seemed brilliant with light. Its very plainness heightened the solemn atmosphere and took away our breath.

Our pilgrimage completed, we walked home again in the dark over the same snow-covered path and, after warming ourselves around the sunken hearth in the main room of the farmhouse, climbed into our beds. Later that morning, as was customary, we welcomed the first day of the year by twisting straw into rope as the year's first labor, symbolizing readiness to work hard throughout the

## Life in the Snow Country

coming months. When this was done, we gathered for our first meal, a special New Year's treat called *o-zoni*, a broth with vegetables and rice cakes that was indescribably delicious.

The New Year holiday was the only time in the year when everyone rested and amused themselves as they liked. Young adults visited one another's houses and played a traditional card game. We smaller children had the time of our lives at a kind of backgammon. Our cards and playing boards were old and worn, but we could imagine nothing more fun than using them and were very sorry when the holiday was over. That we were able to enjoy ourselves completely without things like television makes me extremely aware of the gap between our generation and younger ones.

Even after moving to Tokyo, from time to time I have returned to the village that is the scene of many of my childhood recollections. And until fairly recently the slow old ways were still observed. But now, although not so violently as in the big cities, a wave of change is sweeping into that remote mountain region; one by one, the things I fondly remember are vanishing. It saddens me to think that the pilgrimages to the local shrine on snowy nights, the card and backgammon games, and all the other things associated with New Year's in the country may soon be lost. And when I observe the cool, lifeless way the holiday is kept in the city, I long all the more for the simple people and plain way of life we knew in our mountain village.

## All Things New

On January 1 each year, everything looks new to me. The view from my window is fresher and more vibrant than it was only the day before. I realize, of course, that the mood of the New Year holiday works this change, and I am convinced that a definite break between one year and another makes life more precious and gives it deeper meaning.

But in the dizzying pace of modern times it is hard to use such breaks for leisurely reflection. Contacts with nature, which also stimulate thought about the human condition, have become rare. Our years go by in unfocused busyness. In Japan many people today think of the week-long New Year holiday as a time to do nothing but rest and relax. I feel, however, that it should be a time to reexamine and rediscover the things we overlook in the hustle and bustle of daily life; a time to stimulate in one another the desire for personal improvement.

One way to make these rediscoveries is to assign oneself a topic for thought. It can be a personal topic or something related to society, politics, or the future of one's country. On the morning of January 1, I like to think of the beginning of the universe and the significance of humankind.

The poet and scholar Tachibana Akemi (1812–68) wrote: "On the first of the year, I read first the book of the beginnings of heaven and earth."

That book is the *Kojiki* (Record of Ancient Matters; 712), in which is found this description of the origin of the world: "The land was formless and

## All Things New

floated like oil on water and drifted as soft and shapeless as a jellyfish." From this amorphous state, by stages the earth underwent a series of changes in which volcanoes rose, dense fogs ripped by lightning covered everything, and torrential rains fell. After the turmoil abated, the fresh green earth appeared under a limpid blue sky in which the sun shone brilliantly.

I am astounded by the imaginative powers of ancient people when I realize that the *Kojiki* largely agrees with modern scientific explanations of how the earth was formed. If we use our imaginations in reading the *Kojiki*, we can conjure up images of the pristine world of those times, when winds carried the fragrances of the trees under the deep blue sky and countless stars sparkled at night.

What is the world like today? The atmosphere is polluted; the seas and rivers are clogged with poisonous wastes. City dwellers rarely have an opportunity for more than a glimpse of an occasional star in the night sky. Scientists estimate that human beings have inhabited the earth for a million years or so and that the earth was formed around 4.7 billion years ago. In other words, the age of human beings is less than one five-thousandth of that of the earth.

In comparison with the life of the entire universe, humankind's span is no more than an instant. Yet in that brief time human beings have managed to befoul sky, sea, and earth alike. How foolish such behavior is in beings calling themselves the lords of creation. Today the flaming sun, the luminous moon, and the glittering galaxies that the Buddha would have beheld when he attained enlightenment after meditating under the bo tree at Bodh Gaya are disappearing from our daily lives.

The Buddhist teaching that good causes produce good effects and bad causes produce bad effects helps explain the pollution of our planet. Human beings are paying for the way they destroy natural environments to satisfy their own desires. Though we have brought it on ourselves, when I compare the world today with what I imagine it to have been when it was created, I am struck with the truth of the Buddha's words "Greed is the cause of all suffering." The prosperity and abundance people often speak of are actually no more than euphemisms for naked greed.

Deceived by such superficial thinking and refusing to look back at the havoc already wreaked, humanity continues on its headlong course of destruction. In reflecting on the original condition of the world, I feel chills down my spine as I realize we must avert a catastrophe looming in front of us.

To do that, we must all become beginners again; we must all try to see the future with the freshness and clarity with which we see familiar things on New Year's morning. Then a way will open up before us.

There is an apt saying: "The world begins today." If we let this saying guide our attitude toward our planet, we will see clearly how things ought to be and the directions we must travel to achieve the desired state.

To discover the way, we must become beginners in our hearts and view all things as if they were new. New Year's Day gives us an opportunity to examine our surroundings and lifestyles in this way, which is why I like to spend the morning of January 1 reading and reflecting on accounts of the beginning of the world.

## In the Cold

Each year, many Buddhists undertake a thirty-day period of severe midwinter training that includes such austere practices as standing outdoors and pouring cold water over oneself while praying, invoking the name of Amida Buddha in the harshest weather, and making pilgrimages in the cold. Many of these practices have inspired poets to write haiku. People with other goals also use cold weather to add special impetus to their training programs. For instance, kendo, judo, swimming, and sumo wrestling call for cold-weather regimens, as indeed do courses of instruction in the samisen.

The theory behind all this is that practicing in the cold builds character. We of Rissho Kosei-kai endorse this theory and conduct a yearly winter course of recitation of the Lotus Sutra.

For practical reasons the course lasts only about two weeks, but taking part in it reveals how deeply accustomed we all are to our comfortable modern way of living. The rooms we live and train in are heated. There is little need anymore to struggle against the cold. Consequently, having experienced real cold-weather training for kendo, I think the course is too easy. Nonetheless, it requires an effort to get up at dawn and earnestly read the sutra aloud while fighting to stay awake. But the battle must be won, since one purpose of the course is to overcome drowsiness while joining with many other people in an effort to break out of the habits of ordinary daily life. My first desperate efforts taught me how much discipline is needed just for staying awake.

I further realized that what we were doing was immeasurably easier than the severe disciplines to which the people of the past submitted themselves. When our few days' training were over, I realized that mental attitude, more than physical habit, enables people to overcome hardship.

As soon as I stopped merely reading the sutra and began attempting to understand its meaning as thoroughly as possible and to apply Shakyamuni Buddha's teachings to myself, my drowsiness vanished. I felt refreshed and invigorated. Suddenly making the discovery that this was the meaning of the whole training regimen, I felt as if I had come into contact with the repeated sufferings that people of the past experienced in their attempts to fully understand the Way of the Buddha.

During the winter course, while my wife went about her daily rounds, she sensed the trouble I was having with drowsiness and prepared hot coffee for me every morning. She went on doing so till the end of the course, even though by then I had already overcome drowsiness. I owe part of my victory to my wife, who sensed the cause of my suffering and contributed in her own way to help me overcome it.

*Thoughts on My Family*

## My Father at Home

Many people ask about the way my father, Nikkyo Niwano, lives at home. They say they doubt that he rests or relaxes at home any more than he does when they see him as the busy leader of a religious organization who is always on the move. No doubt they think that his home life is only an extension of his life at work. This impression is especially strong among people who often meet him in relation to his various duties. And they are right, because although we live together, I never see him sitting down, doing nothing, in the daytime.

Since holidays usually coincide with official Rissho Kosei-kai functions, even then he has no time to go for walks or to putter in the garden, as he loves to do. The current growth of leisure activities and the increasingly common five-day work week do not affect him. Innately a hard worker, he is unhappy unless he is constantly moving. His supreme reason for living lies in devoting himself entirely to his tasks. Always being busy helping others is both his greatest pleasure and his optimum regimen.

But after all, he is a human being. When he comes home after a hard day, he immediately becomes the loving grandfather of my four daughters, an ordinary man, whom his grandchildren see as kindly and indulgent. Indeed, my wife and I worry that he will spoil them hopelessly.

To people who inquire about his private life with the idea that he must be aloof or demanding, I say that as far as we at home are concerned, he is neither. I can only say that he is exactly what he seems to be. Indeed, he is simply a member of the family, and one about whom I can recall no intimate anecdotes. I am afraid that attempts to describe him through stories of his home life would only give a distorted impression.

The minute he comes home and changes into kimono, the children clamor around him. When they were younger, he picked up each one and joked and played with them till we all gathered for dinner. If one of them cried or made a fuss during dinner, he picked her up and took her into the living room. Seated there in front of the television set, he cajoled with words and sweets till before long the little offender was sleeping peacefully in his lap. My wife's hands and mine were tied because the children knew that even if we scolded them everything would be all right if they ran to granddad.

Father's great evening pleasure is television. After dinner he sits in front of the set to enjoy dramas, baseball games, or sumo wrestling. Since I

## My Father at Home

am not interested in television, I usually retire to another room and read till bedtime. Consequently I have little chance to compare opinions with him about various programs. But when the subject comes up, he usually praises the educational value of historical dramas in showing how people of other times lived and insists that the learning process must continue throughout life. In other words, he is constantly trying to learn something, to acquire new ideas and information from everything around him, even from watching TV.

He is never formal at home. Since my marriage he has never corrected me or scolded me in any way. I am certain he is not completely satisfied with me, and since I have not yet tasted life's true bitterness, there probably is much he would like to teach me. But he suppresses the desire and merely watches how I develop.

Nor would he feel comfortable with privileged treatment as head of the family. He dislikes claiming such rights. Sometimes he tells stories of the hardships he has experienced in life, but without a trace of self-pity. Instead he seems to regret that his hard times have passed. He mentions these things not tediously or sententiously like some elderly people, but lightheartedly. He enjoys speaking breezily of hardships that people today would have trouble imagining.

Father first came to Tokyo to find a job in 1923, when he was not quite seventeen. His father advised him to look for hard work that paid little. Father took that advice to heart. As a milkman, even in the coldest winter winds he pulled a heavy cart over the longest possible route to earn the money to support his wife and children. His little free time was devoted to disseminating the teachings of the Lotus Sutra. Before that, in the depth of the depression, he pulled a cart loaded with pickles. Of those days he recalls that when people who knew him called out encouraging greetings it brightened his spirit and made his work light.

Hearing this, I realized that all Father's past days were filled with hope, happiness, and sunlight. This is why he never sees hardships as hardships but lives serenely through everything. One thing he has taught me is never to give in but to stand up to whatever life brings.

Another thing I have learned from him is how to entertain the unexpected guests who frequently drop in when he is at home. No matter how much he may want to see the television program being broadcast at the moment, when a guest arrives he rises quickly and changes clothes: he is unwilling for guests, even friends, to see him in his informal kimono. In even this small matter, he demonstrates an old-fashioned respect for decorum. He greets his callers genially and, even when a businesslike approach is appropriate, always puts his visitors at ease with a little friendly small talk.

The consideration for the feelings of others he demonstrates in dealing with callers is extraordinary and extends every day to everyone in our house, sometimes without our realizing it until we are surprised into awareness.

For instance, he long had a habit of rising early and listening to a radio program called "Jinseidokuhon" (Textbook for Life). Then suddenly he stopped getting up early. At first I thought it was a sign of age. But from comments he let slip from time to time, it became apparent he was listening to the program in bed. Not long ago I found out why. It all had to do with our maid. If my father, as head of the house, got up early, no matter how sleepy she might be the maid would have to rise too. To spare her this, Father stopped getting up early and now listens to the program in bed, waiting to rise till he is sure everyone else is up. Thinking about this brings home to me with new force my father's willingness to control his own wishes and to think of everyone else in order to ensure that our home is a warm place where living is pleasant and relaxed.

## Mother, Our Sunlight

Nothing is so difficult as writing about family members. They are always close at hand. One is constantly with them. It would seem easy to jot down interesting anecdotes and random thoughts about them. But when it comes time actually to write, appropriate expressions do not emerge, and no little stories come to mind. Of course, taking our families for granted means that we overlook a great deal. But more hindering is the inability to achieve a well-rounded portrayal through vignettes, thoughts, and anecdotes.

I had that difficulty in writing about Father, and it is even greater in writing about Mother, who is like the sun for my wife and children and my brothers and sisters. She shines radiant above us all the time; but when we try to express our feeling about her, we can think of nothing but platitudes. Still, we do not fully explain what the sun means to us when we say that all the planets in the solar system revolve around it and that it bathes earth in its light and warmth. Thus faced with difficulty, I resolved, as in writing about Father, to limit myself to describing Mother's way of life.

As Father's companion, Mother has struggled with hardship throughout much of her life. A person with great powers of perseverance, she understands what suffering is. And I have often seen her, handkerchief to eye, weeping in sympathy for characters in television dramas and then sharing their joys. Although she realizes these people are fictional, she is nonetheless moved by their emotions. Since she gets about less now than she used to do, she is relatively uninformed about people's affairs. But if someone calls to discuss a problem, Mother listens as if to a relative and then, in a wholehearted effort to help, shares with that person all her knowledge and thoughts on the issue. Indeed, Mother tries so hard that I have sometimes felt sorry for her.

But with the family she is all small talk. Avoiding difficult topics, she laughs, reminisces, and with the greatest delight tells what she has heard.

When it comes to spoiling my children, she does not take a back seat to Father. She is always on their side, even when my wife and I start to scold them roundly for some mischief. When they were small she gave them candy when they cried and she

## Mother, Our Sunlight

took them for walks in the garden when they were restless and bored. All the efforts my wife and I made to train them were as nothing. Though we sometimes exchanged sighs and shrugged our shoulders, we usually came around to seeing that Mother's indulgence too was all for the good. Mother is sunlight to our children, just as she is to the rest of us.

Mother has had her share of hardship, and I sometimes urge her to go away for a good long rest. But she pays no heed. Even on the rare occasions when she does take a holiday, she always returns at once, saying with a sigh of relief: "Home is best." In this she and Father are a perfectly matched pair.

Mother has no particular hobbies or outside interests; her sole pastime is copying the sutras, which she first began doing many years ago. She has already donated to one temple a complete copy she made of the Lotus Sutra. Even though that task is done, she still rises early and, making little noise, continues to copy the sutra practically every day. Once she said of this kind of work: "It's no good doing it mechanically. Each character must be written with a prayer."

Having lived always for her religious faith, Mother finds copying the sutra less a diversion than a kind of discipline, a pursuit through which she hopes to make spiritual progress. Only recently she told me: "Reading the sutra aloud is important, but when I copy it I see all the more how blessed it is and how profound the Buddha's teachings are."

Though Mother is a source of light, warmth, and comfort for us all, she likes to be inconspicuous;

nonetheless she is a mainstay for Father in his busy life as a religious leader. While being our sunlight, Mother also strives hard to instill new energy in herself. In Mother I see the direct application of faith and the diligence that are much more important than theory or doctrine to a person of religion.

## My Long-suffering Wife

Immature though I am, with my wife's assistance since our marriage in 1967 and encouraged by our children's smiling faces, I have become a full-fledged member of society. Unlike me, my wife is bright, open, and talkative. She has what I consider an innate ability to be on friendly terms at once with anyone. I, on the other hand, am shy. It takes a long time for me to get close to people, since even in relaxed situations I tend to listen more than talk. In this my wife and I are opposites. But it is good for a husband and wife to be different, since one can learn from the other while they grow and develop together. Having been helped and educated a great deal by my wife, I am probably more aware of this than most people.

One of the good things about being married is the opportunity it offers to alter and expand one's viewpoint. For instance, every day when I get home I tell my wife about the things I have heard or learned and the people I have met. Generally she listens for a while and then makes comments and states opinions that often startle me and make me see that there are other ways to interpret the issue at hand and that a woman's approach may be very different from a man's.

I respect my wife's understanding of other people's suffering (perhaps she is so understanding because of the suffering she has experienced). Usually people are able to grasp and sympathize fully with the hardships of only close relatives and associates. When I observe that my wife says the right things when listening to other people's misfortunes, I realize that suffering in life is never in vain, even if it does no more than enable us to become sympathetic listeners.

I think the mainstay of married life is caring. Divorce is a common problem for young people today. Of course, each case is different and conditions may be complex; but generalizations can be made. When two people who previously were relative strangers begin to live together as husband and wife, selfishness is likely to emerge. The other person's faults are likely to loom large. No theories or rules can compensate for the failings of both; only caring can. My experience as a married man has taught me that as long as both people care, understanding is possible, mutual selfishness can be overcome, and emotional union can be achieved.

## Our Children

When my daughters were small, they made the whole house their playground. Since no amount of tidying did any good, they were allowed free rein. Everything caught their attention; everything was fascinating.

And usually it was too late to do anything if some prized possession was heedlessly left within their reach. The clutter they left everywhere kept Mother and my wife running about the house all day. But since this too was an important part of growing up, and as long as no danger was involved, I said nothing and allowed the children to do as they wanted.

I may be mistaken, but children who are perfectly good and never misbehave in any way from early childhood seem suppressed. I realize they should not be given total license, but I think that if they are allowed to run a little wild for a time they will grow better and stronger than if they are forced while still small to be good and neat, as if they could be cultivated like bonsai.

Observing my own children always made me reflect on paternal and maternal roles. Eventually I came to understand the importance of winning children's respect and love: respect for the father and love for the mother.

Mothers must do all they can to meet their children's every need. But what, among his many duties, is the prime responsibility of the father? After living with and observing my own four children, I came to the conclusion that earning his children's respect is the most important of a father's duties.

I believe it is shallow to criticize fathers who spend their time at home watching televison, who are out late most nights drinking, or who devote all their spare time to amusements like gambling. Some children deeply revere fathers who have all these faults, whereas fathers who indulge in none of them can still fail to win their children's respect. The important question is not these superficial matters but a man's attitude as a father. In other words, children respect fathers who have objectives in life and devote themselves wholeheartedly to achieving them.

Child-development specialists say that when self-awareness begins budding, at the age of four or five, children begin seeking role models from among the people surrounding them. Mother and father are the most likely models—especially a father who, as head of the house, works responsibly to achieve his aims in life and ensure a happy future for his family.

*Random Thoughts*

## Experiencing Awe

A Japanese proverb has it that four things are awesome: earthquakes, thunder, fires, and father. Never having suffered because of the first three, I do not fear them especially. Though it would be misleading to say I fear my father, I do have a respect akin to awe for his unshakable sincerity and his personality, which has led him to persevere through a life of hardships while serving as spiritual leader for a large number of people. Living and working with him, I find that I respond much more deeply to the example he sets through his own actions than to his corrections or remonstrations.

Though the three awesome phenomena of nature in the Japanese proverb deserve respect, we should also bear in mind the three objects of respect cited in the *Analects* of Confucius: the will of Heaven, great people, and the words of a sage. Confucius himself is supposed to have said that a small person neither knows nor fears the will of Heaven, is too familiar with the great, and despises the words of a sage. A person of diligence in learning and action, on the other hand, fully appreciates all three.

While the Japanese proverb mentions three dangerous phenomena as being worthy of respect, Confucius refers to sources of truth: the will of Heaven—the absolute force that controls the entire universe, including humanity—and great people and sages who, through diligence, have come to understand that force.

Since the things Confucius would have us revere are intangible, people of small capacity fail to fear, respect, or heed them. Instead, regarding the world as existing for their sake alone, such people refuse to recognize the greatness of the great and discard as old-fashioned the precepts inherited from sages of the past. The number of people with such limited vision seems to be increasing recently. That is lamentable, since human beings need to know what to fear and how to put that fear to use for the sake of development and self-improvement.

Too many people today fail to realize the importance of Confucius's observations about the universe and human life.

## Doing What I Dislike Doing

Paradoxically, though I am most uncomfortable when I speak in public, as the days go by I am called on to do more and more public speaking. I am a little more accustomed to writing than I used to be; still I do not really like to do it. Nonetheless, I recently find

## Doing What I Dislike Doing

myself forced to confront a stack of manuscript paper with increasing frequency. Nor is it true that making speeches and writing become easier with practice. The more I try either, the harder I find both.

Others seem to feel the same way. For instance, I read of a famous European lecturer and writer who said that he found public speaking more and more difficult as he became more experienced with it and that he often spent sleepless nights going over the texts of his addresses. From my own experience, this and stories of professional novelists who sit for hours, unable to put anything down on paper, ring very true.

Of all the people I have questioned about these problems, very few have said they like making speeches or find that writing comes easy. But some, such as novelists, have chosen their own path and must endure whatever suffering it entails.

In my case, too, dislike does not relieve me of the responsibility of making public addresses; but I realize that the important thing is to be sincere, even if inept. And I find that if I put my mind to it, I can carry out the task fairly successfully. Nevertheless, whenever I must make a speech, until I begin I am self-absorbed, hesitant, and indescribably tense. I suspect that I shall never be free of these feelings and that most other public speakers, including eloquent ones, share them to one degree or another.

In the case of writing, I find that I procrastinate till the deadline and then sit down to work. Once I start writing, my pen moves smoothly. Recently, probably because I have started emerging bit by bit from the shell into which I tend to shut myself, writing is less difficult.

Human beings find many things distasteful. But unless they forge ahead, they will bog down in hesitation. As the saying goes: "It is more important to act than to think." Plunging into work that is difficult or out of one's ordinary range of abilities will provide experience that can lead to further development and progress.

## Calligraphy

Since I had few calligraphy courses in primary school and high school, I went out into the adult world with no confidence in my ability to write with traditional Japanese brushes and inks. Then some years ago I took up calligraphy seriously.

I wanted to acquire at least the fundamentals of this important Japanese cultural tradition. But I was equally motivated by the shame I felt during trips to outlying districts when members of our organization asked me to sign or write messages on the squares of stiff paper used for such purposes in Japan. On those occasions, unwilling to take brush in hand, I would try to excuse myself by pleading lack of experience or even total ignorance of the art, but always to no avail. No matter how I tried to beg off, I had to comply.

For many years, I most often wrote the word *shoshin*, meaning "beginner's mind." With my lack of confidence, it was the best I could do, and even then I often made mistakes. For example, though the front and back sides of the special paper squares are only slightly different, they are intended for different purposes. On several occasions I wrote on the wrong side. I would like to retrieve all of those mistaken examples of my work and redo them. But it is too late now.

After years of writing "beginner's mind"—finally in a practiced hand—and having entered middle age, I began regular training. I intend to go on with it, keeping my goal in sight, until I am able to produce something approaching true calligraphy.

## A Matchmaker

Though I am inexperienced and feel out of place at gala occasions, people frequently ask me to act as go-between at their weddings. This role involves a number of duties, including making a speech at the wedding reception, describing the backgrounds and personalities of the bride and groom. Since I know most of the young people who ask me, I overcome my hesitations and take on the joyful task.

But unlike my father, who is practiced and impressive in the role, I become excited and make mistakes. For instance, when it comes time for me to speak, I tremble with fear. Afterward I cannot recall what I said. Today brides and grooms are calmer than they once were, but even so, my display of nervousness must be distressing.

Once the ceremonies and reception are over and the young couple are off on their honeymoon, I feel happiness and relief at having carried out my duties. My own calm returns to make me feel better than I can say, and I feel renewed happiness for the couple as they make a new start in life. Only a lot more experience might cure me of nervousness and make me a suitable go-between.

## Driving Safely

I got a driver's license a little over twenty years ago. Every time I sit behind the wheel I think that mental training is more important in safe driving than technical knowledge and skill. The famous nineteenth-century swordsman Miura Heinai said: "People who want to gain a certificate in kendo must become skillful enough to be killed and then, through still harder training, must attain the spiritual state in which they will not be killed. People who have not qualified for kendo certificates are aware of their lack of skill and do not try things that could get them 'killed.' Those who do qualify for a certificate go ahead and take risks and are 'killed' by thousands of people."

Miura's observations apply equally to driving. Most people enthusiastically practice, master the traffic codes, and learn about the structure and working of an automobile before they get a driver's license and then become lax and careless afterward, with the result that accidents occur.

Just as it is difficult to become so good at kendo that others cannot harm you, it is difficult to become so good at driving that you are neither the cause nor the victim of accidents. As long as people with licenses think they can forget about further training and discipline and ignore what Miura called "still harder training," accidents will continue to occur.

I resolved at first not to drive on highways until I had become a perfect driver. I later revised that resolution when I saw that my goal was impossible even if I devoted my whole life to trying to attain it. Nonetheless, I believe that everyone who decides to take up driving ought to have a goal like mine at one time or another.

Recently, speaking on highway safety, a chief of police said: "There is a simple way to make sure you are absolutely never the cause of a traffic accident: never get a driver's license and never drive a car." Some may have thought he was joking, but remembering the words of the kendo expert Miura Heinai, I thought the remark hit the nail on the head.

## Becoming Like Children

I am fond of the artless and unsophisticated, and it is my most cherished wish to be a person who flows freely with the current, mentally resilient enough to rise serenely above all problems and distractions. But real life and its tensions make that impossible.

Largely because of my own personality, I find that while trying to contribute to society through my work, I am unable to devote much of my time to the pursuit of personal goals. Life's pressures often cause me to become tense and bring home to me with renewed force an awareness of the gap between the ideal and the real in life.

Yet as long as I burn with passion for the ideal I pursue, I keep telling myself that I must not give up. The Bible reports Jesus as having said: "Truly, I say to you, unless you turn and become like children, you will never enter the kingdom of heaven" (Matthew 18:3). I hope to remain fervent in my task while becoming like a child in terms of mental flexibility.

Reflecting on artlessness and lack of sophistication recalls to mind a line by the Indian poet and Nobel laureate Rabindranath Tagore: "Man is a born child, his power is the power of growth." Tagore goes on to say something to the effect that children are always suspended in an ageless mystery, unsullied by the dust of history.

## Children's Songs

Children nowadays sing only popular songs or the commercial jingles they hear on the radio or television. I rarely hear them singing the folk and nursery songs I grew up with. Without these songs, children seem to me to be missing something important.

All parents want their children to grow up to be people with refined sensibilities. In order to help my children refine their sensibilities, be appreciative of nature, and be sensitive to beauty and compassion, I still join them in the charming songs of their childhood.

## Children's Songs

These songs deserve to be preserved with fondness because of their intrinsic merits. Not long ago a famous musician from abroad appeared on television to perform several orchestral pieces, one of which struck me as familiar, though I did not recognize its title. Suddenly it dawned on me that it was an orchestral arrangement of a Japanese folk tune, "Seven Children." As it swelled, reached a climax, and then faded away, I realized that this simple piece had been as impressive as all the others. I was happy that the Japanese can boast folk songs of such quality.

The ubiquity of television in today's homes may make it inevitable that pop songs and commercials should oust folk songs from children's minds. But I find this a very sad state of affairs. I want to be at least the kind of parent who can enjoy sharing the warmth and fantasies of old-fashioned nursery songs with his children.

I am certain that children will be more intrigued and fascinated by the richer, more beautiful world of these songs than they could possibly be by senseless commercial jingles. And this fascination might win their interest to the extent that we adults can once again savor the pleasure of hearing bright, childish voices singing these charming songs.

Parents and children ought to be able to participate in the kind of sharing to be enjoyed in the singing of such music.

## The Benefits of Fasting

Since ancient times, fasting has been a part of religious discipline. Many Buddhist sages have found the way to enlightenment through fasting and learning from the ascetic practices followed by Shakyamuni Buddha. As a man of religious faith, I have been concerned to learn what motivated such people and what goals they hoped to attain.

From a book on fasting by a well-known physician, I learned that the goals have been varied. The physician lists thirteen: to receive alms, to show repentance, to make supplication, to seek divine instruction, to achieve union between humankind and the divine, to effect physical therapy, to enhance psychological discipline, to express gratitude for blessings received, to memorialize some event or person, to express grief, to achieve rebirth, to protest, and to further political aims. Many of these goals suggest the deep relation between fasting and religion.

As I read the book, I came to want to experience fasting myself, and thus one spring about twenty-five years ago, I enrolled in a twelve-day program at the Nishishiki Health Center in Tokyo. Actual fasting lasted only three days but nevertheless entailed the hardship of giving up food. During the first four days we gradually reduced the amount of food we ate. After three days of fasting we very gradually increased it. On the first and second days after fasting we had only a little heated water in which rice had been washed; on the third, a very

## The Benefits of Fasting

light rice gruel; on the fourth, a little vegetable soup; and finally, on the last day, a 60 percent portion of an ordinary diet. The twelve days of the whole program were hard, but I learned from the experience.

Since I myself had chosen to undertake the fast, it did not seem so difficult. And the nervous excitement I felt throughout the pre-fast and fast periods kept me from finding them unbearable. But I relaxed after the fast and was attacked by a raging hunger that I tolerated only by gritting my teeth and exercising great self-control. Thinking time would pass faster if I slept, I would go to bed early, lie awake for hours, and then find my eyes wide open before dawn. But this lasted for only a while. Once the worst was over, I actually learned to enjoy the sensation of an empty stomach. I felt physically fresh, and my mind was clear enough to grasp easily passages that had seemed confusing in books read earlier.

According to the book I mentioned earlier, fasting cleanses the stomach and intestines and improves digestive functions to the extent that good health can be maintained on small amounts of food. The cleansing process improves one's health and appearance, clears the head, and vitalizes one's mental functions as well.

In these busy times, many people harm themselves by failing to take good care of their bodies. It would seem advisable for almost everyone to restore good physical condition and clarify the mental and spiritual faculties by occasionally fasting. Even now, I would once again like to sense the freshness and vigor that was my reward for overcoming the hardships of temporarily giving up food entirely.

## Rubbing My Eyes in Wonderment

In the story of Lu Meng in the history of the Wu dynasty (A.D. 222-80) there is a passage in which a man remarks that, after having been away only three days, he could only rub his eyes and stare in wonderment at the progress of a certain great man. In other words, the development of a person who diligently seeks the Way is startlingly fast.

My children's amazingly fast development when they were little made me rub my eyes in astonishment after I had been away from home only a brief while. When I returned after a trip of two or three days or even after a day's work, they often surprised me with the things they had learned and the way they talked about them. I know I sound like the doting father, but most parents must experience the same thing.

The German educator Friedrich Froebel (1782-1852), who originated the kindergarten system, said that it requires more intellectual development for a nursing infant to reach the stage at which it speaks than for a primary school pupil to grow into a scholar of the caliber of Isaac Newton. Froebel based his statement on his observations of the way children grow.

Generally we tend to be unaware of the amazing

process of development leading to the ability to speak. We take it for granted or discount it as only a part of infancy. But in the light of our obligation to rear and cultivate future generations, we should direct more of our concern toward the limitless possibilities of little children. By providing them with all the material they need to grow and develop, we will contribute to the emergence of larger numbers of talented, promising people and thus to a brighter future for humanity.

This is why we must devote sincere efforts to education. I want to raise my own children in such a way that as I watch them healthy and at play, or talk and sing with them, I will constantly be rubbing my eyes in wonderment at the speed of their advancement.